Tacitus

The Madness of Nero

TRANSLATED BY MICHAEL GRANT

PENGUIN EPICS

PENGUIN BOOKS

Published by the Penguin Group
Penguin Books Ltd, 80 Strand, London wc2r orl, England
Penguin Group (USA) Inc., 375 Hudson Street, New York, New York 10014, USA
Penguin Group (Canada), 90 Eglinton Avenue East, Suite 700, Toronto, Ontario, Canada m4p 2y3
(a division of Pearson Penguin Canada Inc.)
Penguin Ireland, 25 St Stephen's Green, Dublin 2, Ireland (a division of Penguin Books Ltd)
Penguin Group (Australia), 250 Camberwell Road, Camberwell, Victoria 3124, Australia
(a division of Pearson Australia Group Pty Ltd)
Penguin Books India Pvt Ltd, 11 Community Centre, Panchsheel Park, New Delhi – 110 017, India
Penguin Group (NZ), cnr Airborne and Rosedale Roads, Albany,
Auckland 1310, New Zealand (a division of Pearson New Zealand Ltd)
Penguin Books (South Africa) (Pty) Ltd, 24 Sturdee Avenue,
Rosebank, Johannesburg 2196, South Africa

Penguin Books Ltd, Registered Offices: 80 Strand, London wc2r orl, England

www.penguin.com

The Annals of Imperial Rome first published in Penguin Classics 1956
Revised editions published 1959, 1971, 1973, 1975, 1977, 1989
The Twelve Caesars first published in Penguin Classics 1957
Revised edition published 1979
These extracts published in Penguin Books 2006

3

Translation of The Annals of Imperial Rome copyright © Michael Grant Publications Ltd,
1956, 1959, 1971, 1973, 1975, 1977, 1989
Translation of The Twelve Caesars copyright © Robert Graves 1957;
revisions copyright © Michael Grant Publications Ltd, 1979
All rights reserved

The moral right of the translator has been asserted

Typeset by Rowland Phototypesetting Ltd, Bury St Edmunds, Suffolk
Printed in England by Clays Ltd, St Ives plc

isbn–13: 978–0–141–02686–2
isbn–10: 0–141–02686–3

Contents

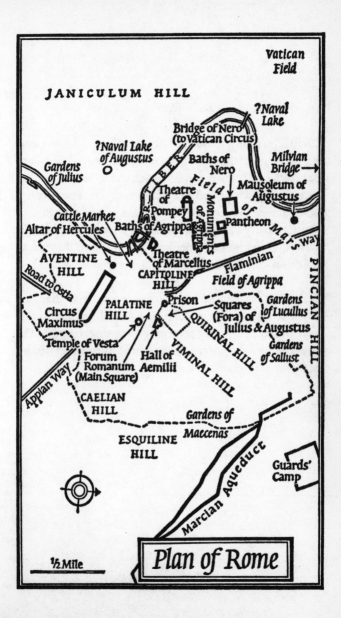

Plan of Rome

Note

Tacitus probably wrote *The Annals of Imperial Rome* during the reign of the emperor Trajan (AD 98–117). Substantial parts of the text have not survived, including that part dealing with Nero's reign after AD 66. The extracts here exclude the sections on the wars in Armenia, Britain and Germany and focus on life in Rome. Tacitus' text breaks off before the rebellions against Nero that led to his death (Suetonius gives a gripping account of this).

Following the murder of his wife Messalina, Claudius has married Agrippina. The position of his son by his previous marriage, Britannicus, is now threatened by the rival claim to the succession of Nero, Agrippina's son by her own previous marriage.

The Murder of the Emperor Claudius

In the following year the consuls were Faustus Cornelius Sulla Felix and Lucius Salvius Otho Titianus. Lucius Arruntius Furius Scribonianus was now exiled for inquiring from astrologers about the emperor's death. The charge was also extended to his mother, Vibia, recalcitrant (it was alleged) against her earlier sentence of expulsion. The fact that Scribonianus' father, Lucius Arruntius Camillus Scribonianus, had rebelled in Dalmatia was cited by the emperor to illustrate his mercy in again sparing this disaffected family. But the exile did not survive long. Did Scribonianus die naturally or by poison? People spread their own beliefs. The senate passed a severe, but futile, decree banning astrologers from Italy.

The emperor, in a speech, praised senators who voluntarily abandoned their rank through poverty. Those however who, by not retiring, showed shamelessness as well as indigence were expelled. Next Claudius proposed to the senate that women marrying slaves should be penalized. It was decided that the penalty for such a lapse should be enslavement, if the man's master did not know, and the status of an ex-slave if he did. The emperor revealed that this proposal was due to Pallas; to whom accordingly rewards of an honorary praetorship and fifteen million sesterces were proposed by the consul-designate Marcius Barea Soranus. Publius Cornelius

Lentulus Scipio (II) added the suggestion that Pallas should be given the nation's thanks because, though descended from Arcadian kings, he preferred the national interests to his antique lineage, and let himself be regarded as one of the emperor's servants. Claudius reported that Pallas was content with that distinction only, and preferred not to exceed his former modest means. So the senate's decree was engraved in letters of bronze; it loaded praises for old-world frugality on a man who had once been a slave and was now worth three hundred million sesterces.

Pallas' brother, the knight Antonius Felix, who was the governor of Judaea, showed less moderation. Backed by vast influence, he believed himself free to commit any crime. However, the Jews had shown unrest and had rioted when Gaius ordered the erection of his own statue in the Temple. Gaius died before the order had been carried out, but there remained fears that a later emperor would repeat it. Moreover, Felix stimulated outbreaks by injudicious disciplinary measures. His bad example was imitated by Ventidius Cumanus, who controlled part of the province. For Judaea was divided: the Samaritans came under Felix and the Galileans under Ventidius.

These tribes had a long-standing feud, which their contempt for their present rulers now allowed to rage unrestrained. They ravaged each other's territory with invading robber gangs, setting traps for one another and sometimes openly clashing, and then depositing their thefts and plunder with the Roman officials. At first the two men were pleased. Then, as the situation became graver, they intervened with troops – which suffered reverses. War would have flamed up throughout the province if the imperial governor of Syria had not intervened.

Jews who had ventured to kill Roman soldiers were executed without hesitation. The cases of Cumanus and Felix were more embarrassing. For Claudius, learning the causes of the revolt, had empowered Quadratus to deal with these officials himself. He displayed Felix as one of the judges, his position on the bench being intended to silence his accusers. Cumanus was condemned for the irregularities of both. Then the Judaean province was peaceful again.

Shortly afterwards the wild Cilician tribes of the Cietae, which had often caused disturbances, fortified a mountainous position under their chief Troxoboris, and descended from it upon the cities and the coast. There they boldly attacked cultivators, townsmen, and often traders and ship-owners. They besieged Anemurium, and defeated a cavalry force under Curtius Severus sent to its relief from Syria; for the rough ground impeded cavalry operations and favoured the Cilicians who were on foot. Finally Antiochus Epiphanes IV of Commagene, the dependent monarch who controlled the coast, by offering inducements to the rank and file and tricking their leader, split the native forces, and after executing the chief and a few of his associates pardoned and pacified the rest.

A tunnel through the mountain between the Fucine Lake and the river Liris had now been completed. To enable a large crowd to see this impressive achievement a naval battle was staged on the lake itself, like the exhibition given by Augustus on his artificial lake adjoining the Tiber, though his ships and combatants had been fewer. Claudius equipped warships manned with nineteen thousand combatants, surrounding them with a circle of rafts to prevent their escape. Enough space in the middle, however, was left for energetic rowing, skilful steering, charging, and all the incidents of a sea-battle. On the rafts were stationed double companies of the Guard and other units, behind ramparts from which they could shoot catapults and stone-throwers. The rest of the lake was covered with the decked ships of the marines.

The coast, the slopes, and the hill-tops were thronged like a theatre by innumerable spectators, who had come from the neighbouring towns and even from Rome itself – to see the show or pay respects to the emperor. Claudius presided in a splendid military cloak, with Agrippina in a mantle of cloth of gold. Though the fighters were criminals they fought like brave men. After much blood-letting, they were spared extermination.

After the display, the waterway was opened. But careless construction became evident. The tunnel had not been sunk to the bottom of the lake or even halfway down. So time had to be allowed for the deepening of the channel. A second crowd was assembled, this time to witness an infantry battle fought by gladiators on pontoons. But, to the horror of banqueters near the lake's outlet, the force of the out-rushing water swept away everything in the vicinity – and the crash and roar caused shock and terror even farther afield. Agrippina took advantage of the emperor's alarm to accuse Narcissus, the controller of the project, of illicit profits. He retorted by assailing her dictatorial, feminine excess of ambition.

Next year, when the consuls were Decimus Junius Silanus Torquatus and Quintus Haterius Antoninus, Nero, aged sixteen, married the emperor's daughter Octavia. Eager to make a brilliant name as learned and eloquent, Nero successfully backed Ilium's application to be exempted from all public burdens, fluently recalling the descent of Rome from Troy and of the Julii from Aeneas, and other more or less mythical traditions. Nero's advocacy also secured for the settlement of Bononia, which had been burnt down, a grant of ten million sesterces. Next the Rhodians – continually liberated or subjected in accordance with their services in foreign wars, or lapses into disorder at home – recovered their freedom. And Phrygian Apamea, overwhelmed by an earthquake, was granted remission of taxes for five years.

But Agrippina's intrigues were still driving Claudius to the most brutal behaviour. Titus Statilius Taurus (II), famous for his wealth, had gardens which she coveted. So she broke him. The prosecutor she used as her instrument was Tarquitius Priscus. When Taurus was governor of Africa, Tarquitius had been his deputy; now that they were back he accused Taurus of a few acts of extortion but more especially of magic. Unable any longer to endure undeserved humiliation by a lying accuser, the defendant, without awaiting the senate's verdict, took his own life. The senate, however, so detested the informer that they expelled him – although Agrippina was his supporter.

On several occasions this year the emperor was heard saying that the decisions of knights who were his agents should be as valid as his own judgements. And in case these should be regarded as chance utterances, the senate decreed on the subject in more detailed and comprehensive terms than hitherto. The divine Augustus had conferred jurisdiction on those who governed Egypt, their judgements to rank with those of senatorial officials. Later, in other provinces and in Rome as well, knights were ceded many judicial cases hitherto heard by governors and praetors respectively. Now Claudius handed over to the knights all the powers which had so often caused rioting and fighting, as, for instance, when the laws of Gaius Sempronius Gracchus (I) gave them a monopoly of places on the Bench and the law of Quintus Servilius Caepio restored them to the senate. This was the principal issue in the fighting between Marius and Sulla. In earlier days, however, the struggle had been between classes, and the results extorted applied to a whole class. Julius Caesar's protégés, Gaius Oppius and Lucius Cornelius Balbus (I), were the first individuals important enough to decide issues of peace and war. Later names of powerful members of the order, such as Gaius Matius and Publius Vedius Pollio, are not worth mentioning since Claudius now gave even ex-slaves, placed in control of his personal estates, equal authority with himself and the law.

Next he proposed to exempt Cos from taxation. In a lengthy discourse about its ancient history, he said that its first inhabitants had been Argives – or perhaps Coeus, the father of the goddess Latona; then Aesculapius had brought the art of healing, which had achieved remarkable distinction among his descendants. The emperor indicated their names and the periods at which each had lived. Then he added that a member of the same family was his own doctor, Gaius Stertinius Xenophon: in response to whose petition the people of Cos would in future be exempted from all taxation, holding their island as a sacred place, and serving the god alone. Claudius might, of course, have recalled their frequent assistance to Rome, and the victories they had shared with us. But he preferred not to disguise behind external arguments the favour which, with his usual indulgence, he had conceded to an individual.

The Byzantines, on the other hand, when their protests against oppressive burdens were given a hearing, reviewed all their services to Rome. Beginning with their treaty with Rome at the time of our war against the king of Macedonia known, owing to his dubious origin, as pseudo-Philip, they then recounted their services against Antiochus III, Perseus, and Aristonicus, their assistance to Marcus Antonius Creticus in the Pirate War, to Sulla, Lucius Licinius Lucullus, and Pompey, and finally, in more recent times, to the Caesars. The reason for these services had been their situation at a convenient crossing-point for generals and their armies and supplies. For the Greeks had founded Byzantium at the narrowest part of the strait between Europe and Asia. When they asked Pythian Apollo where to found a city, the oracle replied 'opposite the land of the blind'. This riddle referred to

Chalcedon, whose inhabitants had arrived in the region earlier and had seen the superb site first but chosen an inferior one. Byzantium had originally been rich and prosperous. It has a fertile soil and a productive sea, since great numbers of fish, coming from the Black Sea and scared by shelving rocks under the surface on the winding Asiatic coast, swim away from it into the harbours on the European side. But subsequently financial burdens became oppressive; and now they begged for exemption or alleviation. The emperor supported them, arguing that their exhaustion from recent wars in Thrace and the Crimean Bosphorus entitled them to relief. A remission of tribute was granted for five years.

In the following year the consuls were Marcus Asinius Marcellus and Manius Acilius Aviola. A series of prodigies indicated changes for the worse. Standards and soldiers' tents were set on fire from the sky. A swarm of bees settled on the pediment of the Capitoline temple. Half-bestial children were born, and a pig with a hawk's claws. A portent, too, was discerned in the losses suffered by every official post: a quaestor, aedile, tribune, praetor, and consul had all died within a few months. Agrippina was particularly frightened – because Claudius had remarked in his cups that it was his destiny first to endure his wives' misdeeds, and then to punish them. She decided to act quickly.

First, however, out of feminine jealousy, she destroyed Domitia Lepida,* who regarded herself as Agrippina's equal in nobility – she was daughter of Antonia (I), and

---

* Domitia Lepida was the mother of Messalina.

grand-niece of Augustus; cousin once removed of Agrippina; and sister of Agrippina's former husband Cnaeus Domitius Ahenobarbus. In beauty, age, and wealth there was little between the two women. Moreover both were immoral, disreputable, and violent, so they were as keen rivals in vicious habits as in the gifts bestowed on them by fortune. But their sharpest issue was whether aunt or mother should stand first with Nero. Lepida sought to seduce his youthful character by kind words and indulgence. Agrippina on the other hand, employed severity and menaces – she could give her son the empire, but not endure him as emperor.

However, the charge against Lepida was attempting the life of the empress by magic, and disturbing the peace of Italy by failing to keep her Calabrian slave-gangs in order. On these charges she was sentenced to death – in spite of vigorous opposition by Narcissus.* His suspicions of Agrippina continually grew deeper. 'Whether Britannicus or Nero comes to the throne,' he was said to have told his friends, 'my destruction is inevitable. But Claudius has been so good to me that I would give my life to help him. The criminal intentions for which Messalina was condemned with Gaius Silius have re-emerged in Agrippina. With Britannicus as his successor the emperor has nothing to fear. But the intrigues of his stepmother in Nero's interests are fatal to the imperial house – more ruinous than if I had said nothing about her predecessor's unfaithfulness. And once more there is unfaithfulness. Agrippina's lover is Pallas. *That* is the

---

* Claudius' Secretary-General.

final proof that there is nothing she will not sacrifice to imperial ambition – neither decency, nor honour, nor chastity.'

Talking like this, Narcissus would embrace Britannicus and pray he would soon be a man. With hands outstretched – now to the boy, now to heaven – he besought that Britannicus might grow up and cast out his father's enemies, and even avenge his mother's murderers. Then Narcissus' anxieties caused his health to fail. He retired to Sinuessa, to recover his strength in its mild climate and health-giving waters.

Agrippina had long decided on murder. Now she saw her opportunity. Her agents were ready. But she needed advice about poisons. A sudden, drastic effect would give her away. A gradual, wasting recipe might make Claudius, confronted with death, love his son again. What was needed was something subtle that would upset the emperor's faculties but produce a deferred fatal effect. An expert in such matters was selected – a woman called Locusta, recently sentenced for poisoning but with a long career of imperial service ahead of her. By her talents, a preparation was supplied. It was administered by the eunuch Halotus who habitually served the emperor and tasted his food.

Later, the whole story became known. Contemporary writers stated that the poison was sprinkled on a particularly succulent mushroom. But because Claudius was torpid – or drunk – its effect was not at first apparent; and an evacuation of his bowels seemed to have saved him. Agrippina was horrified. But when the ultimate stakes are so alarmingly large, immediate disrepute is brushed aside. She had already secured the complicity of the emperor's doctor Xenophon; and now she called him in. The story is that, while pretending to help Claudius to vomit, he put a feather dipped in a quick poison down his throat. Xenophon knew that major crimes, though hazardous to undertake, are profitable to achieve.

The senate was summoned. Consuls and priests offered prayers for the emperor's safety. But meanwhile his already lifeless body was being wrapped in blankets and poultices. Moreover, the appropriate steps were being taken to secure Nero's accession. First Agrippina, with heart-broken demeanour, held Britannicus to her as though to draw comfort from him. He was the very image of his father, she declared. By various devices she prevented him from leaving his room and likewise detained his sisters, Claudia Antonia and Octavia. Blocking every approach with troops, Agrippina issued frequent encouraging announcements about the emperor's health, to maintain the Guards' morale and await the propitious moment forecast by the astrologers.

At last, at midday on October the thirteenth, the palace gates were suddenly thrown open. Attended by Sextus Afranius Burrus, commander of the Guard, out came Nero to the battalion which, in accordance with regulations, was on duty. At a word from its commander, he was cheered and put in a litter. Some of the men are said to have looked round hesitantly and asked where Britannicus was. However, as no counter-suggestion was made, they accepted the choice offered them. Nero was then conducted into the Guards' camp. There, after saying a few words appropriate to the occasion – and promising gifts on the generous standard set by his father – he was hailed as emperor. The army's decision was followed by senatorial decrees. The provinces, too, showed no hesitation.

Claudius was voted divine honours, and his funeral was modelled on that of the divine Augustus – Agrippina imitating the grandeur of her great-grandmother Livia, the first Augusta. But Claudius' will was not read, in case his preference of stepson to son should create a public impression of unfairness and injustice.

The Fall of Agrippina

The first casualty of the new reign was the governor of Asia, Marcus Junius Silanus (II). His death was treacherously contrived by Agrippina, without Nero's knowledge. It was not provoked by any ferocity of temper. Silanus was lazy, and previous rulers had despised him – Gaius used to call him 'the Golden Sheep'. But Agrippina was afraid he would avenge her murder of his brother, Lucius Junius Silanus Torquatus (I). Popular gossip, too, widely suggested that Nero, still almost a boy and emperor only by a crime, was less eligible for the throne than a mature, blameless aristocrat who was, like himself, descended from the Caesars. For Silanus was a great-great-grandson of the divine Augustus – and this still counted. So he was murdered. The act was done by a knight, Publius Celer, and a former slave, Helius, the emperor's agents in Asia. Without the precautions necessary to maintain secrecy, they administered poison to the governor at dinner.

Equally hurried was the death of Claudius' ex-slave Narcissus. I have described his feud with Agrippina. Imprisoned and harshly treated, the threat of imminent execution drove him to suicide. The emperor, however, was sorry: Narcissus' greed and extravagance harmonized admirably with his own still latent vices.

Other murders were meant to follow. But the emperor's tutors, Sextus Afranius Burrus and Lucius Annaeus Seneca, prevented them. These two men, with a unanimity rare among partners in power, were, by different methods, equally influential. Burrus' strength lay in soldierly efficiency and seriousness of character, Seneca's in amiable high principles and his tuition of Nero in public speaking. They collaborated in controlling the emperor's perilous adolescence; their policy was to direct his deviations from virtue into licensed channels of indulgence. Agrippina's violence, inflamed by all the passions of ill-gotten tyranny, encountered their united opposition.

She, however, was supported by Pallas, who had ruined Claudius by instigating his incestuous marriage and disastrous adoption. But Nero was not disposed to obey slaves. Pallas' surly arrogance, anomalous in a man of servile origin, disgusted him. Nevertheless, publicly, Agrippina received honour after honour. When the escort-commander made the customary request for a password, Nero gave: 'The best of mothers.' The senate voted her two official attendants and the Priesthood of Claudius.

For Claudius was declared a god. A public funeral was to come first. On the day of the funeral the emperor pronounced his predecessor's praises. While he recounted the consulships and Triumphs of the dead man's ancestors, he and his audience were serious. References to Claudius' literary accomplishments too, and to the absence of disasters in the field during his reign, were favourably received. But when Nero began to talk of his stepfather's foresight and wisdom, nobody could help laughing.

Yet the speech, composed by Seneca, was highly polished – a good example of his pleasant talent, which admirably suited contemporary taste. Older men, who spent their leisure in making comparisons with the past, noted that Nero was the first ruler to need borrowed eloquence. The dictator Julius Caesar had rivalled the greatest orators. Augustus spoke with imperial fluency and spontaneity. Tiberius was a master at weighing out his words – he could express his thoughts forcibly, or he could be deliberately obscure. Even Gaius' mental disorders had not weakened his vigorous speech; Claudius' oratory, too, was graceful enough, provided it was prepared. But from early boyhood Nero's mind, though lively, directed itself to other things – carving, painting, singing, and riding. Sometimes, too, he wrote verses, and thereby showed he possessed the rudiments of culture.

Sorrow duly counterfeited, Nero attended the senate and acknowledged its support and the army's backing. Then he spoke of his advisers, and of the examples of good rulers before his eyes. 'Besides, I bring with me no feud, no resentment or vindictiveness,' he asserted. 'No civil war, no family quarrels, clouded my early years.' Then, outlining his future policy, he renounced everything that had occasioned recent unpopularity. 'I will not judge every kind of case myself,' he said, 'and give too free rein to the influence of a few individuals by hearing prosecutors and defendants behind my closed doors. From my house, bribery and favouritism will be excluded. I will keep personal and State affairs separate. The senate is to preserve its ancient functions. By applying to the consuls, people from Italy and the senatorial provinces may have access to its tribunals. I myself will look after the armies under my control.'

Moreover, these promises were implemented. The senate decided many matters. They forbade advocates to receive fees or gifts. They excused quaestors-designate from the obligation to hold gladiatorial displays. Agrippina objected to this as a reversal of Claudius' legislation. Yet it was carried – although the meeting was convened in the Palatine, and a door built at the back so that she could stand behind a curtain unseen, and listen. Again, when an Armenian delegation was pleading before Nero, she was just going to mount the emperor's dais and sit beside him. Everyone was stupefied. But Seneca instructed Nero to advance and meet his mother. This show of filial dutifulness averted the scandal.

[. . .]

In the same year the emperor requested the senate to authorize statues of his late father Cnaeus Domitius Ahenobarbus and his guardian Asconius Labeo. He declined an offer to erect statues of himself in solid gold or silver. The senate had decreed that future years should begin in December, the month of his birth. But he retained the old religious custom of starting the year on January Ist. He refused to allow the prosecution of a Roman knight, Julius Densus, for favouring Britannicus – or of a junior senator, Carrinas Celer, who was accused by a slave. Consul in the next year, Nero exempted his colleague Lucius Antistius Vetus from swearing allegiance, like the other officials, to the emperor's acts. The senate praised this vigorously; they hoped that if his youthful heart were elated by popularity for minor good deeds he might turn to greater ones. Then he showed leniency by readmitting to the senate Plautius Lateranus, who had been expelled for adultery with Messalina. Nero pledged himself to clemency in numerous speeches; Seneca put them into his mouth, to display his own talent or demonstrate his high-minded guidance.

Agrippina was gradually losing control over Nero. He fell in love with a former slave Acte. His confidants were two fashionable young men, Marcus Salvius Otho,* whose father had been consul, and Claudius Senecio, son of a former imperial slave. Nero's secret, surreptitious, sensual meetings with Acte established her ascendancy. When Nero's mother finally discovered, her opposition was fruitless. Even his older friends were not displeased to see his appetites satisfied by a common girl with no grudges. Destiny, or the greater attraction of forbidden pleasures, had alienated him from his aristocratic and virtuous wife Octavia, and it was feared that prohibition of his affair with Acte might result in seductions of noblewomen instead.

Agrippina, however, displayed feminine rage at having an ex-slave as her rival and a servant girl as her daughter-in-law, and so on. She refused to wait until her son regretted the association, or tired of it. But her violent

---

* Who was to become emperor for a few months in AD 69.

scoldings only intensified his affection for Acte. In the
end, deeply in love, he became openly disobedient to his
mother and turned to Seneca – one of whose intimates,
Annaeus Serenus, had screened the first stages of the
liaison by lending his own name as the ostensible donor
of the presents which Nero secretly gave Acte. Agrippina
now changed her tactics, and indulgently offered the
privacy of her own bedroom for the relaxations natural
to Nero's age and position. She admitted that her strictness had been untimely, and placed her resources –
which were not much smaller than his own – at his
disposal. This change from excessive severity to extravagant complaisance did not deceive Nero – and it alarmed
his friends, who urged him to beware of the tricks of this
always terrible and now insincere woman.

One day Nero was looking at the robes worn by the
resplendent wives and mothers of former emperors.
Picking out a jewelled garment, he sent it as a present to
his mother – a generous, spontaneous gift of a greatly
coveted object. But Agrippina, instead of regarding this
as an addition to her wardrobe, declared that her son
was doling out to her a mere fraction of what he owed
her – all else but this one thing was kept from her. Some
put a sinister construction on her words.

Nero, exasperated with the partisans of this female
conceit, deposed Pallas from the position from which,
since his appointment by Claudius, he had virtually
controlled the empire. As the ex-slave left the palace with
a great crowd of followers, the emperor penetratingly
commented 'Pallas is going to swear himself out of his
state functions'. In fact, Pallas had substituted for that

customary oath of high officials a stipulation that there should be no investigations of his past conduct, and that his account with the State should be regarded as balanced.

Agrippina was alarmed; her talk became angry and menacing. She let the emperor hear her say that Britannicus was grown up and was the true and worthy heir of his father's supreme position – now held, she added, by an adopted intruder, who used it to maltreat his mother. Unshrinkingly she disclosed every blot on that ill-fated family, without sparing her own marriage and her poisoning of her husband. 'But heaven and myself are to be thanked,' she added, 'that my stepson is alive! I will take him to the Guards' camp. Let them listen to Germanicus' daughter pitted against the men who claim to rule the whole human race – the cripple Burrus with his maimed hand, and Seneca, that deportee with the professorial voice!' Gesticulating, shouting abuse, she invoked the deified Claudius, the spirits of the Silani below – and all her own unavailing crimes.

This worried Nero. As the day of Britannicus' fourteenth birthday approached, he pondered on his mother's violent behaviour – also on Britannicus' character, lately revealed by a small indication which had gained him wide popularity. During the amusements of the Saturnalia the young men had thrown dice for who should be king, and Nero had won. To the others he gave various orders causing no embarrassment. But he commanded Britannicus to get up and come into the middle and sing a song. Nero hoped for laughter at the boy's expense, since Britannicus was not accustomed even to sober parties, much less to drunken ones. But Britannicus composedly sang a poem implying his displacement from his father's home and throne. This aroused sympathy – and in the frank atmosphere of a nocturnal party, it was unconcealed. Nero noticed the feeling against himself, and hated Britannicus all the more.

Though upset by Agrippina's threats, he could not find a charge against his stepbrother or order his execution openly. Instead, he decided to act secretly – and ordered poison to be prepared. Arrangements were entrusted to a colonel of the Guard, Julius Pollio, who was in charge of the notorious convicted poisoner Locusta. It had earlier been ensured that Britannicus' attendants should be unscrupulous and disloyal. His tutors first administered the poison. But it was evacuated, being either too weak or too diluted for prompt effectiveness. Impatient at the slowness of the murder, Nero browbeat the colonel and ordered Locusta to be tortured. They thought of nothing but public opinion, he complained; they safeguarded themselves and regarded his security as a secondary consideration. Then they swore that they would produce effects as rapid as any sword-stroke; and in a room adjoining Nero's bedroom, from well-tried poisons, they concocted a mixture.

It was the custom for young imperial princes to eat with other noblemen's children of the same age at a special, less luxurious table, before the eyes of their relations: that is where Britannicus dined. A selected servant habitually tasted his food and drink. But the murderers thought of a way of leaving this custom intact without giving themselves away by a double death. Britannicus was handed a harmless drink. The taster had tasted it; but Britannicus found it too hot, and refused it. Then cold water containing the poison was added. Speechless, his whole body convulsed, he instantly ceased to breathe.

His companions were horrified. Some, uncomprehending, fled. Others, understanding better, remained rooted in their places, staring at Nero. He still lay back unconcernedly – and he remarked that this often happened to epileptics; that Britannicus had been one since infancy; soon his sight and consciousness would return. Agrippina tried to control her features. But their evident consternation and terror showed that, like Britannicus' sister Octavia, she knew nothing. Agrippina realized that her last support was gone. And here was Nero murdering a relation. But Octavia, young though she was, had learnt to hide sorrow, affection, every feeling. After a short silence the banquet continued.

Britannicus was cremated the night he died. Indeed, preparations for his inexpensive funeral had already been made. As his remains were placed in the Field of Mars, there erupted a violent storm. It was widely believed that the gods were showing their fury at the boy's murder – though even his fellow-men generally condoned it, arguing that brothers were traditional enemies and that the empire was indivisible. A number of contemporary writers assert that for a considerable time previously Nero had corrupted his victim. If so, his death might have seemed to come none too soon, and be the lesser outrage of the two.

Such was this hurried murder of the last of the Claudians, physically defiled, then poisoned right among the religious emblems on the table, before his enemy's eyes – without time even to give his sister a farewell kiss. Nero justified the hasty funeral by an edict recalling the traditional custom of withdrawing untimely deaths from the public gaze and not dwelling on them with eulogies and processions. Now that he had lost his brother's help, he added, all his hopes were centred on his country; senate and people must give all the greater support to their emperor, the only remaining member of his family, exalted by destiny. Then he distributed lavish gifts to his closest friends. Some were shocked when, at such a juncture, men of ethical pretensions accepted his distribution of town and country mansions like loot. Others thought they had no choice since the emperor, with his guilty conscience, hoped for impunity if he could bind everyone of importance to himself by generous presents.

However, no generosity could mollify his mother. She became Octavia's supporter. Constantly meeting her own friends in secret, Agrippina outdid even her natural greed in grasping funds from all quarters to back her designs. She was gracious to officers, and attentive to such able and high-ranking noblemen as survived. She seemed to be looking round for a Party, and a leader for it. Learning this, Nero withdrew the military bodyguard which she had been given as empress and retained as the emperor's mother, and also the German Guardsmen by which, as an additional compliment, it had recently been strengthened. Furthermore, he terminated her great receptions, by giving her a separate residence in the mansion formely occupied by Antonia (II). When he visited her there, he would bring an escort of staff-officers, hurriedly embrace her, and leave.

Veneration of another person's power, if it is ill-supported, is the most precarious and transient thing in the world. Agrippina's house was immediately deserted. Her only visitors and comforters were a few women, there because they loved her – or hated her. One of them was Junia Silana, whose separation from her husband Gaius Silius (II) by Messalina I have described. Noble, beautiful, and immoral, she had long been an intimate friend of Agrippina. Recently, however, an unspoken enmity had arisen between them, because Agrippina had deterred a young nobleman, Titus Sextius Africanus, from marrying Silana by describing her as immoral and past her prime. Agrippina did not want him for herself, but wanted to keep him from obtaining the childless Silana's wealth.

Silana now saw her chance of revenge. She put up two of her dependants, Iturius and Calvisius, to prosecute Agrippina. They avoided the old, frequently heard charges of her mourning Britannicus' death or proclaiming Octavia's wrongs. Instead they accused her of inciting Rubellius Plautus to revolution. This man, through his mother, possessed the same relationship to the divine Augustus as Nero did. Agrippina, the allegation was, proposed to marry Plautus and control the empire again. Nero's aunt Domitia – who was Agrippina's deadly rival – had a freed slave Atimetus who heard this story from the two prosecutors and urged the ballet-dancer Paris (another of Domitia's former slaves) to go speedily and divulge the plot to the emperor, in sensational terms.

It was late at night when Paris entered. Nero had long been drinking. This was the time Paris usually came, to enliven the emperor's dissipations. Tonight, however, Paris wore a gloomy expression; and he told his story in detail. The emperor, listening in terror, resolved to kill his mother, to kill Plautus, and also to depose Burrus from the command of the Guard, as being a supporter and nominee of Agrippina. One historian, Fabius Rusticus, claims that Nero had actually written a letter of appointment to a proposed successor of Burrus, Gaius Caecina Tuscus, and that it was only through Seneca's influence that Burrus retained his post. But this authority favours Seneca, whose friendship had made his career; and two other writers, Pliny the Elder and Cluvius Rufus, report no doubts of Burrus' loyalty. (My plan is to indicate such individual sources only when they differ. When they are unanimous, I shall follow them without citation.)

Nero was so alarmed and eager to murder his mother that he only agreed to be patient when Burrus promised that, if she was found guilty, she should die. But Burrus pointed out that everyone must be given an opportunity for defence – especially a parent; and that at present there were no prosecutors but only the report of one man, from a household unfriendly to her. Nero should reflect, he added, that it was late and they had spent a convivial night, and that the whole story had an air of recklessness and ignorance.

This calmed the emperor's fears. Next morning, Burrus visited Agrippina to acquaint her with the accusation and tell her she must refute it or pay the penalty. Burrus did this in Seneca's presence; certain ex-slaves were also there as witnesses. Burrus named the charges and the accusers, and adopted a menacing air. But Agrippina displayed her old spirit. 'Junia Silana has never had a child,' she said, 'so I am not surprised she does not understand a mother's feelings! For mothers change their sons less easily than loose women change their lovers. If Silana's dependants Iturius and Calvisius, after exhausting their means, can only repay the hag's favours by becoming accusers, is that a reason for darkening my name with my son's murder, or loading the emperor's conscience with mine?

'As for Domitia, I should welcome her hostility if she were competing with me in kindness to my Nero – instead of concocting melodramas with her lover Atimetus and the dancer Paris. While I was planning Nero's adoption and promotion to consular status and designation to the consulship, and all the other preparations for his accession, she was beautifying her fishponds at her beloved Baiae.

'I defy anyone to convict me of tampering with city police or provincial loyalty, or of inciting slaves and ex-slaves to crimes. If Britannicus had become emperor could I ever have survived? If Rubellius Plautus or another gained the throne and became my judge, there would be no lack of accusers! For then I should be charged, not with occasional indiscretions – outbursts of uncontrollable love – but with crimes which no one can pardon except a son!'

Agrippina's listeners were touched, and tried to calm

her excitement. But she demanded to see her son. To him, she offered no defence, no reminder of her services. For the former might have implied misgivings, the latter reproach. Instead she secured rewards for her supporters – and revenge on her accusers. Junia Silana, on the other hand, was exiled, her dependants Iturius and Calvisius expelled, Atimetus executed. Paris played too important a part in the emperor's debaucheries to be punished. Rubellius Plautus was left unnoticed – for the present. Publius Anteius, appointed imperial governor of Syria, was put off by various devices and finally kept in Rome. Faenius Rufus was given control of the food supply, Arruntius Stella given the Games projected by the emperor, and Tiberius Claudius Balbillus made imperial governor of Egypt.

Pallas and Burrus were charged with conspiring to give the empire to Faustus Cornelius Sulla Felix, because of his great name and marriage link with Claudius, whose daughter Claudia Antonia was his wife. The accusation originated with a certain Paetus, notorious for acquiring confiscated properties from the Treasury. His story was clearly untrue. But Pallas' innocence did not cause much satisfaction because of the disgust provoked by his arrogance. For when certain ex-slaves in his household were denounced as his accomplices, Pallas replied that all orders in his home were given by nods or waves of the hand – when more detailed instructions were required he wrote them, to avoid personal contact. Burrus, though himself among the accused, was one of the judges, and pronounced acquittal. The informer was banished, and his records unearthing forgotten debts to the Treasury were burnt.

At the end of the year the battalion of the Guard customarily present at the Games was withdrawn. The intention was to give a greater impression of freedom, to improve discipline by removing the Guardsmen from the temptations of public displays, and to test whether the public would behave respectably without their restraint.

The temples of Jupiter and Minerva were struck by lightning. The emperor consulted diviners and on their recommendation conducted a purification of the city.

The consuls for the following year were Quintus Volusius Saturninus and Publius Cornelius Lentulus Scipio (II). The year was a time of peace abroad, but disgusting excesses by Nero in Rome. Disguised as a slave, he ranged the streets, brothels, and taverns with his friends, who pilfered goods from shops and assaulted wayfarers. Their identity was unsuspected: indeed, as marks on his face testified, Nero himself was struck. When it became known that the waylayer was the emperor, attacks on distinguished men and women multiplied. For, since disorderliness was tolerated, pseudo-Neros mobilized gangs and behaved similarly, with impunity. Rome by night came to resemble a conquered city.

A senator called Julius Montanus, who had not yet held office, assaulted by the emperor in the dark, hit back vigorously. But then Montanus recognized his assailant and apologized. However his apology was interpreted as a slur, and he was forced to commit suicide. Yet the incident diminished Nero's boldness. In future he surrounded himself with soldiers and masses of gladiators, and these, while holding aloof from minor semi-private brawls, intervened forcibly whenever the victims showed vigorous resistance.

In the theatre, there were brawls between gangs favouring rival ballet-dancers. Nero converted these disorders into serious warfare. For he waived penalties and offered prizes – watching in person, secretly and on many occasions even openly. Finally, however, public animosities and fears of worse disturbances left no alternative but to expel these dancers from Italy and station troops in the theatre again.

About this time the senate discussed the offences of former slaves. It was demanded that patrons should be empowered to re-enslave undeserving ex-slaves. The proposal had widespread support. But the consuls did not dare to put the motion without consulting the emperor, to whom they wrote stating the senate's view. Since his advisers, though few, were divided, Nero hesitated to give a ruling. One side denounced the disrespectfulness of liberated slaves. 'It goes to such lengths,' they said, 'that former slaves confront their patron with the choice of yielding them their rights by legal argument, as equals, or by force. Freed slaves even lift their hands to strike their former master – and sarcastically urge their own punishment. For all that an injured patron may do is to send his freed slave away beyond the hundredth milestone – to the Campanian beaches! In all other respects the two men are legally equal and identical. Patrons ought to be given a weapon which cannot be disregarded. It would be no hardship for the liberated to have to keep their freedom by the same respectful behaviour which won it for them. Indeed, blatant offenders ought to be enslaved again, so as to frighten the ungrateful into obedience.'

The opposite argument went thus: 'The guilty few ought to suffer, but not to the detriment of freed slaves' rights in general. For ex-slaves are everywhere. They provide the majority of the voters, public servants, attendants of officials and priests, watchmen, firemen. Most knights, many senators, are descended from former slaves. Segregate the freed – and you will only show how few free-born there are! When our ancestors fixed degrees of rank, they were right to make everyone free. Besides, two sorts of liberation were instituted to leave room for second thoughts or favour. Some were liberated "by the wand", those who were not remained half-slaves. Slave-owners ought to consider individual merits, but be slow to grant what is irrevocable.'

This opinion prevailed. Nero wrote asking the senate to give separate consideration to every charge by a patron, but not to diminish the rights of ex-slaves in general. Soon afterwards his aunt Domitia was deprived of the patronage of her former slave Paris, ostensibly on legal grounds. He was pronounced free-born, on the orders of the emperor – whose reputation suffered thereby.

Nevertheless there were still signs of a free country. A dispute arose between a praetor, Vibullius, and a tribune, Antistius Sosianus, because the latter had ordered the release of some of the disorderly followers of ballet-dancers. The praetor had imprisoned these hangers-on, and the senate backed him, censuring the tribune for irregularity. They also forbade tribunes to encroach on the authority of praetors and consuls, or to summon Italian litigants to Rome in cases where local settlement was practicable. The consul-designate Lucius Calpurnius Piso (V) added proposals that tribunes should not exercise their powers in their own homes, and that fines imposed by them should not be entered in the Treasury records for four months, during which time objections could be lodged for adjudication by the consuls. The powers of aediles, too, were curtailed, limits being fixed to the sums which 'curule' aediles and aediles of the people could distrain or fine. Moreover a quaestor in charge of the Treasury, Helvidius Priscus (II), was quarrelling with a tribune, Obultronius Sabinus, who charged him with over-rigorous compulsory sales of poor men's property. Thereupon the emperor transferred the Treasury and public accounts from quaestors to commissioners who were experienced former praetors. The control of the Treasury has undergone numerous changes. Augustus entrusted it to commissioners selected by the senate. Later, when improper canvassing was suspected, they were chosen by lot from the praetors. But the lot could fall on incompetent men, so this arrangement too was short-lived. Claudius returned the post to quaestors. However, thinking they might prove inactive through fear of giving offence, he promised them exceptional promotion. But the young men lacked the maturity for so important a first post.

A governor of Sardinia, Vipsanius Laenas, was found guilty of fraudulence (also in this year). However, a governor of Achaia, Cestius Proculus, charged by the Cretans with extortion, was exonerated. The fleet-commander at Ravenna, Publius Palpellius Clodius Quirinalis, who had inflicted his savagery and debauchery on Italy as if it were the humblest of subject territories, poisoned himself to forestall condemnation. Caninius Rebilus, outstanding in legal learning and wealth, escaped the miseries of invalid old age by opening his veins. No one had thought he had the courage for this, because of his notorious effeminacy. Lucius Volusius Saturninus (II) also died, leaving a distinguished reputation and a great fortune, honestly won. He had lived to ninety-three and avoided the malevolence of every emperor.

Next year, when the consuls were Nero (for the second time) and Lucius Calpurnius Piso (V), little worth recording occurred, except in the eyes of historians who like filling their pages with praise of the foundations and beams of Nero's huge amphitheatre in the Field of Mars. But that is material for official gazettes, whereas it has traditionally been judged fitting to Rome's grandeur that its histories should contain only important events. Drafts of ex-soldiers were sent to two Italian settlements, Capua and Nuceria. The city population were given a bonus of four hundred sesterces a head. Forty million sesterces were paid into the Treasury to maintain public credit. The 4 per cent tax on the purchase of slaves was waived (though its removal was a fiction, since the tax was only shifted to the dealers, who increased their prices accordingly).

The emperor also published instructions that no provincial official, in his province, should give shows of gladiators or wild beasts, or any other display. For hitherto this ostensible generosity had been as oppressive to provincials as extortion, the governors' intention being to win partisans to screen their irregularities. The senate also passed a punitive and precautionary measure. If a man was murdered by his slaves, those liberated by his will – if they were in the house – were to be executed with the rest.

At this time a former consul Lurius Varus, formerly convicted of extortion, was restored to his rank. The distinguished lady Pomponia Graecina, wife of Aulus Plautius – whose official ovation for British victories I have mentioned – was charged with foreign superstition and referred to her husband for trial. Following ancient tradition he decided her fate and reputation before her kinsmen, and acquitted her. But her long life was continuously unhappy. For after the murder, by Messalina's intrigues, of her relative Livia Julia – daughter of Drusus – she wore mourning and grieved unceasingly for forty years. This escaped punishment under Claudius, and thereafter gave her prestige.

The same year witnessed several prosecutions. Publius Celer was accused by the province of Asia. He, as I have mentioned, had been the murderer of his governor Marcus Junius Silanus (II) – a great enough crime to overshadow his other misdeeds. Nero could not acquit him. Instead he protracted the case until Celer died of old age. Cossutianus Capito was indicted by the Cilicians. This vicious and disreputable individual believed he could behave as outrageously in his province as in Rome. Defeated, however, by determined prosecutors, he abandoned his defence and was condemned under the extortion law. The Lycians claimed damages from Titus Clodius Eprius Marcellus. But his intrigues were so effective that some of his accusers were exiled for endangering an innocent man.

Nero's colleague in his third consulship was Marcus Valerius Messalla Corvinus (II), whose great-grandfather, the orator of the same name, a few old men remembered as consular colleague of Nero's great-great-grandfather the divine Augustus. The reputation of Messalla's distinguished family was now buttressed by an annual grant of half a million sesterces to enable him to support his poverty honestly. The emperor also conferred annuities on two other senators, Aurelius Cotta and Quintus Haterius Antoninus, though both had squandered their inherited fortunes by extravagance.

[. . .]

For these achievements [the wars in Armenia] Nero was officially hailed as victor. The senate decreed thanksgivings. They voted the emperor statues, arches, and a succession of consulships. The days of the victory and its announcement were to rank as festivals. Following further extravagant decrees of the same sort, Gaius Cassius Longinus – who had supported the other honours – observed that if the gods were to be thanked worthily for their favours the whole year was too short for their thanksgivings: so a distinction should be made between religious festivals and working days on which people might perform religious duties without neglecting mundane ones.

Now came the condemnation of Publius Suillius Rufus. He had earned much hatred in his stormy career. Nevertheless his fall brought discredit upon Seneca. Under Claudius the venal Suillius had been formidable. Changed times had not brought him as low as his enemies wished. Indeed, he envisaged himself as aggressor rather than suppliant. It was to suppress him – so it was said – that the senate had revived an old decree under the Cincian law, penalizing advocates who accepted fees. Suillius protested abusively, reviling Seneca with characteristic ferocity and senile outspokenness.

'Seneca hates Claudius' friends,' said Suillius. 'For under Claudius he was most deservedly exiled! He only understands academic activities and immature youths. So he envies men who speak out vigorously and unaffectedly for their fellow-citizens. I was on Germanicus' staff – while Seneca was committing adultery in his house! Is the acceptance of rewards a dependant offers voluntarily, for an honourable job, a worse offence than seducing imperial princesses? What branch of learning, what philosophical school, won Seneca three hundred million sesterces during four years of imperial friendship? In Rome, he entices into his snares the childless and their legacies. His huge rates of interest suck Italy and the provinces dry. I, on the other hand, have worked for my humble means. I will endure prosecution, trial, and everything else rather than have my lifelong efforts wiped out by this successful upstart!'

There were people to tell Seneca of these words, or exaggerated versions of them. Accusers were found. They charged Suillius with fleecing the provincials as governor of Asia, and embezzling public funds. The prosecution was granted a year for investigation. Meanwhile it was thought quicker to begin with charges relating to Rome – for which witnesses were available. They accused Suillius of forcing a former consul, Quintus Pomponius Secundus, into civil war by his savage indictments, driving Livia Julia, daughter of Drusus, and Poppaea Sabina to their deaths, striking down Decimus Valerius Asiaticus and two other ex-consuls, Quintus Lutetius Lusius Saturninus and Cornelius Lupus, and convicting masses of knights – in a word, all the brutalities of Claudius.

Suillius' defence was that he had invariably acted not on his own initiative but on the emperor's orders. But Nero cut him short, declaring that his father Claudius had never insisted on any prosecutions – his papers proved it. Suillius then alleged instructions from Messalina. But this defence too broke down. For why (it was asked) had just Suillius, and no one else, been selected to speak for that barbarous harlot? – the instrument of atrocities, the man who was paid for crimes and then blamed them on others, must be punished.

Half his estate was confiscated. His son, Marcus Suillius Nerullinus, and granddaughter were allowed the other half, as well as what they had inherited from their mother and grandmother. Suillius himself was exiled to the Balearic islands. Neither ordeal nor aftermath broke his spirit. His retirement was known to be sustained by comfortable self-indulgence. When accusers, relying on Suillius' unpopularity, prosecuted his son for extortion, the emperor felt vengeance was satisfied and vetoed the proceedings.

At about this time the tribune Octavius Sagitta, madly in love with a married woman called Pontia, paid her vast sums to become his mistress and then to leave her husband. He promised to marry her, and secured a similar promise from her. But once she was free she procrastinated, pleading her father's opposition and evading her promise – a richer husband now being in prospect. Octavius remonstrated, threatened, and appealed – his reputation and money were both gone (he said), and his life, all that he had left, he put in her hands. But she remained unmoved.

He pleaded for one night – as a consolation and to help him control himself in future. The night was fixed. Pontia had a maid in attendance who knew of the affair. Octavius arrived with a former slave. Under his clothes was a dagger. Love and anger took their course. They quarrelled, pleaded, insulted each other, made it up. For part of the night they made love. Then, ostensibly carried away by passion, he stabbed the unsuspecting woman with his dagger. A maid ran in and fell wounded by him. Then he fled.

When day came the murder was discovered. They were proved to have been together; the murderer was unmistakable. The ex-slave, however, claimed that the action was his, undertaken to avenge his patron's wrongs. Many were convinced by his devotion. But the maid recovered from her wound and revealed the truth.

Octavius was charged before the consuls by his victim's father. He ceased to be tribune and was condemned by senatorial decree and under the law of murder.

An equally conspicuous case of immorality in the same year brought grave national disaster. There was at Rome a woman called Poppaea. Friendship with Sejanus had ruined her father, Titus Ollius, before he held office, and she had assumed the name of her brilliant maternal grandfather, Gaius Poppaeus Sabinus, of illustrious memory for his consulship and honorary Triumph. Poppaea had every asset except goodness. From her mother, the loveliest woman of her day, she inherited distinction and beauty. Her wealth, too, was equal to her birth. She was clever and pleasant to talk to. She seemed respectable. But her life was depraved. Her public appearances were few; she would half-veil her face at them, to stimulate curiosity (or because it suited her). To her, married or bachelor bedfellows were alike. She was indifferent to her reputation – yet insensible to men's love, and herself unloving. Advantage dictated the bestowal of her favours.

While married to a knight called Rufrius Crispinus – to whom she had borne a son – she was seduced by Marcus Salvius Otho, an extravagant youth who was regarded as peculiarly close to Nero. Their liaison was quickly converted into marriage. Otho praised her charms and graces to the emperor. This was either a lover's indiscretion or a deliberate stimulus prompted by the idea that joint possession of Poppaea would be a bond reinforcing Otho's own power. As he left the emperor's table he was often heard saying he was going to his wife, who had brought him what all men want and only the fortunate enjoy – nobility and beauty.

Under such provocations, delay was brief. Poppaea obtained access to Nero, and established her ascendancy. First she used flirtatious wiles, pretending to be unable to resist her passion for Nero's looks. Then, as the emperor fell in love with her, she became haughty, and if he kept her for more than two nights she insisted that she was married and could not give up her marriage. 'I am devoted to Otho. My relations with him are unique. His character and way of living are both fine. *There* is a man for whom nothing is too good. Whereas you, Nero, are kept down because the mistress you live with is a servant, Acte. What a sordid, dreary, menial association!'

Otho lost his intimacy with the emperor. Soon he was excluded from Nero's receptions and company. Finally, to eliminate his rivalry from the Roman scene, he was made governor of Lusitania. There, until the civil war, he lived moderately and respectably – enjoying himself in his spare time, officially blameless.

At this juncture Nero stopped trying to justify his criminal misdeeds. He particularly distrusted Faustus Cornelius Sulla Felix, whose stupidity he wrongly interpreted as well-concealed cunning. This suspicion was intensified by the fabrication of an old former imperial slave Graptus, familiar with the palace since Tiberius' reign. At this time the Milvian Bridge was notorious for its night resorts. Nero used to go there; he could enjoy himself more riotously outside the city. On his way home by the Flaminian road one night, a few young revellers, typical of the times, caused groundless alarm among his attendants. 'There had been a plot to attack Nero!' lied Graptus. 'Only a providential detour to the Gardens of Sallust had saved him – and the plotter was Sulla!' No slave or dependant of Sulla was identified, and his wholly timid and despicable character was incapable of such an attempt. However, he was treated as if proved guilty, exiled, and confined to Massilia.

This year Puteoli sent two opposing delegations to the senate, one from the town council and one from the other citizens. The council complained of public disorderliness, and the populace of embezzlement by officials and leading men. There had been riots, with stone-throwing and threatened arson. Gaius Cassius Longinus was appointed to prevent armed warfare and find a solution. But the town could not stand his severity, and at his own request the task was transferred to two brothers, Publius Sulpicius Scribonius Proculus and Sulpicius Scribonius Rufus. They were allocated a battalion of the Guard, fear of which – supplemented by a few executions – restored harmony.

The senate also passed a decree authorizing the city of Syracuse to exceed the numbers allowed at gladiatorial displays. This would be too insignificant to mention had not the opposition of Publius Clodius Thrasea Paetus given his critics a chance to attack his attitude. 'If,' they said, 'Thrasea believes Rome needs a free senate, why does he pursue such trivial matters? Why does he not argue one way or the other about questions of war and peace, taxation, legislation, and other matters of national importance? When a senator is called upon to speak, he may speak about anything and demand a motion about it. Is the prevention of extravagance at Syracusan shows the only reform we need? Is everything else in the empire as good as if Thrasea and not Nero were its ruler? If significant matters are passed over and ignored, surely trivialities ought to be left alone.' Thrasea, asked by his friends to justify himself, replied that it was not through ignorance of the general situation that he offered criticism on such a subject, but because he respectfully credited the senate with understanding that men who attended to these details would not fail to show attention to important matters also.

In this year there were persistent public complaints against the companies farming indirect taxes from the government. Nero contemplated a noble gift to the human race: he would abolish every indirect tax. But the senators whom he consulted, after loudly praising his noble generosity, restrained his impulse. They indicated that the empire could not survive without its revenues, and that abolition of the indirect customs dues would be followed by demands to abolish direct taxation also. Many companies for collecting indirect taxes, they recalled, had been established by consuls and tribunes in the freest times of the Republic; since then such taxation had formed part of the efforts to balance income and expenditure. But Nero's advisers agreed that tax-collectors' acquisitiveness must be restrained, to prevent novel grievances from discrediting taxes long endured uncomplainingly.

So the emperor's orders were these. Regulations governing each tax, hitherto confidential, were to be published. Claims for arrears were to lapse after one year. Praetors at Rome, governors in the provinces, must give special priority to cases against tax-collectors. Soldiers were to remain tax-free except on what they sold. There were other excellent provisions too. But they were soon evaded – though the abolition of certain illegal exactions invented by tax-collectors, such as the 2½ per cent and 2 per cent duties, is still valid. Overseas transportation of grain was facilitated, and it was decided to exempt merchant ships from assessment and property-tax.

At this juncture two ex-governors of Africa, Quintus Sulpicius Camerinus and Marcus Pompeius Silvanus, were tried by the emperor and acquitted. Camerinus was charged not with embezzlement but with brutal acts towards a few individuals; Silvanus was beset by a crowd of accusers who requested time to collect witnesses. But he insisted on an immediate hearing, and being rich, old, and childless, was successful. Moreover, he outlived the legacy-hunters whose scheming had secured his acquittal!

[. . .]

The fig-tree called 'Ruminalis', in the Place of Assembly, which 830 years earlier had sheltered the babies Romulus and Remus, suffered in this year. Its shoots died and its trunk withered. This was regarded as a portent. However, it revived, with fresh shoots.

When the new year came, and Gaius Vipstanus Apronianus and Gaius Fonteius Capito (II) became consuls, Nero ceased delaying his long-meditated crime.

The longer his reign lasted, the bolder he became. Besides, he loved Poppaea more every day. While Agrippina lived, Poppaea saw no hope of his divorcing Octavia and marrying her. So she nagged and mocked him incessantly. He was under his guardian's thumb, she said – master neither of the empire nor of himself. 'Otherwise,' she said, 'why these postponements of our marriage? I suppose my looks and victorious ancestors are not good enough. Or do you distrust my capacity to bear children? Or the sincerity of my love?

'No! I think you are afraid that, if we were married, I might tell you frankly how the senate is downtrodden and the public enraged by your mother's arrogance and greed. If Agrippina can only tolerate daughters-in-law who hate her son, let me be Otho's wife again! I will go anywhere in the world where I only need hear of the emperor's humiliations rather than see them – and see you in danger, like myself!' This appeal was reinforced by tears and all a lover's tricks. Nero was won. Nor was there any opposition. Everyone longed for the mother's domination to end. But no one believed that her son's hatred would go as far as murder.

According to one author, Cluvius Rufus, Agrippina's passion to retain power carried her so far that at midday, the time when food and drink were beginning to raise Nero's temperature, she several times appeared before her inebriated son all decked out and ready for incest. Their companions observed sensual kisses and evilly suggestive caresses. Seneca, supposing that the answer to a woman's enticements was a woman, called in the ex-slave Acte. She feared for Nero's reputation – and for her own safety. Now she was instructed to warn Nero that Agrippina was boasting of her intimacy with her son, that her boasts had received wide publicity, and that the army would never tolerate a sacrilegious emperor.

Another writer, Fabius Rusticus, agrees in attributing successful intervention to Acte's wiles, but states that the desires were not Agrippina's but Nero's. But the other authorities support the contrary version. So does the tradition. That may be because Agrippina really did intend this monstrosity. Or perhaps it is because no sexual novelty seemed incredible in such a woman. In her earliest years she had employed an illicit relationship with Marcus Aemilius Lepidus (V) as a means to power. Through the same ambition she had sunk to be Pallas' mistress. Then, married to her uncle, her training in abomination was complete. So Nero avoided being alone with her. When she left for her gardens or country mansions at Tusculum and Antium, he praised her intention of taking a holiday.

Finally, however, he concluded that wherever Agrippina was she was intolerable. He decided to kill her. His only doubt was whether to employ poison, or the dagger, or violence of some other kind. Poison was the first choice. But a death at the emperor's table would not look fortuitous after Britannicus had died there. Yet her criminal conscience kept her so alert for plots that it seemed impracticable to corrupt her household. More-over, she had strengthened her physical resistance by a preventive course of antidotes. No one could think of a way of stabbing her without detection. And there was another danger: that the selected assassin might shrink from carrying out his dreadful orders.

However, a scheme was put forward by Anicetus, an ex-slave who commanded the fleet at Misenum. In Nero's boyhood Anicetus had been his tutor; he and Agrippina hated each other. A ship could be made, he now said, with a section which would come loose at sea and hurl Agrippina into the water without warning. Nothing is so productive of surprises as the sea, remarked Anicetus; if a shipwreck did away with her, who could be so unreasonable as to blame a human agency instead of wind and water? Besides, when she was dead the emperor could allot her a temple and altars and the other public tokens of filial duty.

This ingenious plan found favour. The time of year, too, was suitable, since Nero habitually attended the festival of Minerva at Baiae. Now he enticed his mother there. 'Parents' tempers must be borne!' he kept announcing. 'One must humour their feelings.' This was to create the general impression that they were friends again, and to produce the same effect on Agrippina. For women are naturally inclined to believe welcome news.

As she arrived from Antium, Nero met her at the shore. After welcoming her with outstretched hands and embraces, he conducted her to Bauli, a mansion on the bay between Cape Misenum and the waters of Baiae. Some ships were standing there. One, more sumptuous than the rest, was evidently another compliment to his mother, who had formerly been accustomed to travel in warships manned by the imperial navy. Then she was invited out to dinner. The crime was to take place on the ship under cover of darkness. But an informer, it was said, gave the plot away; Agrippina could not decide whether to believe the story, and preferred a sedan-chair as her conveyance to Baiae.

There her alarm was relieved by Nero's attentions. He received her kindly, and gave her the place of honour next himself. The party went on for a long time. They talked about various things; Nero was boyish and intimate – or confidentially serious. When she left, he saw her off, gazing into her eyes and clinging to her. This may have been a final piece of shamming – or perhaps even Nero's brutal heart was affected by his last sight of his mother, going to her death.

But heaven seemed determined to reveal the crime. For it was a quiet, star-lit night and the sea was calm. The ship began to go on its way. Agrippina was attended by two of her friends. One of them, Crepereius Gallus, stood near the tiller. The other, Acerronia, leant over the feet of her resting mistress, happily talking about Nero's remorseful behaviour and his mother's re-established influence. Then came the signal. Under the pressure of heavy lead weights, the roof fell in. Crepereius was crushed, and died instantly. Agrippina and Acerronia were saved by the raised sides of their couch, which happened to be strong enough to resist the pressure. Moreover, the ship held together.

In the general confusion, those in the conspiracy were hampered by the many who were not. But then some of the oarsmen had the idea of throwing their weight on one side, to capsize the ship. However, they took too long to concert this improvised plan, and meanwhile others brought weight to bear in the opposite direction. This provided the opportunity to make a gentler descent into the water. Acerronia ill-advisedly started crying out, 'I am Agrippina! Help, help the emperor's mother!' She was struck dead by blows from poles and oars and whatever ship's gear happened to be available. Agrippina herself kept quiet and avoided recognition. Though she was hurt – she had a wound in the shoulder – she swam until she came to some sailing-boats. They brought her to the Lucrine lake, from which she was taken home.

There she realized that the invitation and special compliment had been treacherous, and the collapse of her ship planned. The collapse had started at the top, like a stage-contrivance. The shore was close by, there had been no wind, no rock to collide with. Acerronia's death and her own wound also invited reflection. Agrippina decided that the only escape from the plot was to profess ignorance of it. She sent an ex-slave Agerinus to tell her son that by divine mercy and his lucky star she had survived a serious accident. The messenger was to add, however, that despite anxiety about his mother's dangerous experience Nero must not yet trouble to visit her – at present rest was what she needed. Meanwhile, pretending unconcern, she cared for her wound and physical condition generally. She also ordered Acerronia's will to be found and her property sealed. Here alone no pretence was needed.

To Nero, awaiting news that the crime was done, came word that she had escaped with a slight wound – after hazards which left no doubt of their instigator's

identity. Half-dead with fear, he insisted she might arrive
at any moment. 'She may arm her slaves! She may whip
up the army, or gain access to the senate or Assembly,
and incriminate me for wrecking and wounding her and
killing her friends! What can I do to save myself?' Could
Burrus and Seneca help? Whether they were in the plot
is uncertain. But they were immediately awakened and
summoned.

For a long time neither spoke. They did not want to
dissuade and be rejected. They may have felt matters
had gone so far that Nero had to strike before Agrippina,
or die. Finally Seneca ventured so far as to turn to Burrus
and ask if the troops should be ordered to kill her.
He replied that the Guard were devoted to the whole
imperial house and to Germanicus' memory; they would
commit no violence against his offspring. Anicetus, he
said, must make good his promise. Anicetus unhesitat-
ingly claimed the direction of the crime. Hearing him,
Nero cried that this was the first day of his reign – and the
magnificent gift came from a former slave! 'Go quickly!'
he said. 'And take men who obey orders scrupulously!'

Agrippina's messenger arrived. When Nero was told,
he took the initiative, and staged a fictitious incrimination. While Agerinus delivered his message, Nero
dropped a sword at the man's feet and had him arrested
as if caught red-handed. Then he could pretend that his
mother had plotted against the emperor's life, been
detected, and – in shame – committed suicide.

Meanwhile Agrippina's perilous adventure had become known. It was believed to be accidental. As soon
as people heard of it they ran to the beach, and climbed

on to the embankment, or fishing-boats nearby. Others
waded out as far as they could, or waved their arms. The
whole shore echoed with wails and prayers and the din
of all manner of inquiries and ignorant answers. Huge
crowds gathered with lights. When she was known to
be safe, they prepared to make a show of rejoicing.

But a menacing armed column arrived and dispersed
them. Anicetus surrounded her house and broke in.
Arresting every slave in his path, he came to her bedroom
door. Here stood a few servants – the rest had been
frightened away by the invasion. In her dimly lit room
a single maid waited with her. Agrippina's alarm had
increased as nobody, not even Agerinus, came from her
son. If things had been well there would not be this
terribly ominous isolation, then this sudden uproar. Her
maid vanished. 'Are you leaving me, too?' called Agrippina. Then she saw Anicetus. Behind him were a naval
captain and lieutenant named Herculeius and Obaritus
respectively. 'If you have come to visit me,' she said,
'you can report that I am better. But if you are assassins,
I know my son is not responsible. He did not order his
mother's death.' The murderers closed round her bed.
First the captain hit her on the head with a truncheon.
Then as the lieutenant was drawing his sword to finish
her off, she cried out: 'Strike here!' – pointing to her
womb. Blow after blow fell, and she died.

So far accounts agree. Some add that Nero inspected
his mother's corpse and praised her figure; but that is
contested. She was cremated that night, on a dining
couch, with meagre ceremony. While Nero reigned, her
grave was not covered with earth or enclosed, though

later her household gave her a modest tomb beside the road to Misenum, on the heights where Julius Caesar's mansion overlooks the bay beneath. During the cremation one of her former slaves, Mnester (II), stabbed himself to death. Either he loved his patroness, or he feared assassination.

This was the end which Agrippina had anticipated for years. The prospect had not daunted her. When she asked astrologers about Nero, they had answered that he would become emperor but kill his mother. Her reply was, 'Let him kill me – provided he becomes emperor!' But Nero only understood the horror of his crime when it was done. For the rest of the night, witless and speechless, he alternately lay paralysed and leapt to his feet in terror – waiting for the dawn which he thought would be his last. Hope began to return to him when at Burrus' suggestion the colonels and captains of the Guard came and cringed to him, with congratulatory handclasps for his escape from the unexpected menace of his mother's evil activities. Nero's friends crowded to the temples. Campanian towns nearby followed their lead and displayed joy by sacrifices and deputations.

Nero's insincerity took a different form. He adopted a gloomy demeanour, as though sorry to be safe and mourning for his parent's death. But the features of the countryside are less adaptable than those of men; and Nero's gaze could not escape the dreadful view of that sea and shore. Besides, the coast echoed (it was said) with trumpet blasts from the neighbouring hills – and wails from his mother's grave. So Nero departed to Neapolis.

He wrote the senate a letter. Its gist was that Agerinus, a confidential ex-slave of Agrippina, had been caught with a sword, about to murder him, and that she, conscious of her guilt as instigator of the crime, had paid the penalty. He added older charges. 'She had wanted to be co-ruler – to receive oaths of allegiance from the Guard, and to subject senate and public to the same humiliation. Disappointed of this, she had hated all of them – army, senate and people. She had opposed gratuities to soldiers and civilians alike. She had contrived the deaths of distinguished men.' Only with the utmost difficulty, added Nero, had he prevented her from breaking into the senate-house and delivering verdicts to foreign envoys. He also indirectly attacked Claudius' régime, blaming his mother for all its scandals. Her death, he said, was providential. And he even called the shipwreck a happy accident. For even the greatest fool could not believe it accidental – or imagine that one shipwrecked woman had sent a single armed man to break through the imperial guards and fleets. Here condemnation fell not on Nero, whose monstrous conduct beggared criticism, but on Seneca who had composed his self-incriminating speech.

Nevertheless leading citizens competed with complimentary proposals – thanksgivings at every shrine; annual games at Minerva's Festival (during which the discovery of the plot had been staged); the erection in the senate-house of gold statues of Minerva and (beside her) the emperor; the inclusion of Agrippina's birthday among ill-omened dates. It had been the custom of Publius Clodius Thrasea Paetus to pass over flatteries in silence or with curt agreement. But this time he walked out of the senate – thereby endangering himself without bringing general freedom any nearer.

Many prodigies occurred. A woman gave birth to a snake. Another woman was killed in her husband's arms by a thunderbolt. The sun suddenly went dark. All fourteen city-districts were struck by lightning. But these portents meant nothing. So little were they due to the gods that Nero continued his reign and his crimes for years to come.

However, to intensify his mother's unpopularity and indicate his increased leniency now she had gone, he brought back two eminent women, Junia Calvina and Calpurnia (II), and two former praetors, Valerius Capito and Licinius Gabolus, whom she had exiled. He even permitted Lollia Paulina's ashes to be brought home, and a tomb erected. He also allowed back Junia Silana's two dependants, Iturius and Calvisius, whom he had recently banished. Silana herself had died at Tarentum, having returned from her distant exile when Agrippina, whose malevolence had struck her down, became less vindictive – or less powerful.

Nero lingered in the cities of Campania. His return to Rome was a worrying problem. Would the senate be obedient? Would the public cheer him? Every bad character (and no court had ever had so many) reassured him that Agrippina was detested, and that her death had increased his popularity. They urged him to enter boldly and see for himself how he was revered. Preceding him – as they had asked to – they found even greater enthusiasm than they had promised. The people marshalled in their tribes were out to meet him, the senators were in their gala clothes, wives and children drawn up in lines by sex and age. Along his route there were tiers of seats as though for a Triumph. Proud conqueror of a servile nation, Nero proceeded to the Capitol and paid his vows.

Then he plunged into the wildest improprieties, which vestiges of respect for his mother had hitherto not indeed repressed, but at least impeded.

Nero and His Helpers

Nero had long desired to drive in four-horse chariot races. Another equally deplorable ambition was to sing to the lyre, like a professional. 'Chariot-racing,' he said, 'was an accomplishment of ancient kings and leaders – honoured by poets, associated with divine worship. Singing, too, is sacred to Apollo: that glorious and provident god is represented in a musician's dress in Greek cities, and also in Roman temples.'

There was no stopping him. But Seneca and Burrus tried to prevent him from gaining both his wishes by conceding one of them. In the Vatican valley, therefore, an enclosure was constructed, where he could drive his horses, remote from the public eye. But soon the public were admitted – and even invited; and they approved vociferously. For such is a crowd: avid for entertainment, and delighted if the emperor shares their tastes. However, this scandalous publicity did not satiate Nero, as his advisers had expected. Indeed, it led him on. But if he shared his degradation, he thought it would be less; so he brought on to the stage members of the ancient nobility whose poverty made them corruptible. They are dead, and I feel I owe it to their ancestors not to name them. For though they behaved dishonourably, so did the man who paid them to offend (instead of not to do so). Well-known knights, too, he induced by huge presents to offer their services in the arena. But gifts from the man who can command carry with them an obligation.

However, Nero was not yet ready to disgrace himself on a public stage. Instead he instituted 'Youth Games'. There were many volunteers. Birth, age, official career did not prevent people from acting – in Greek or Latin style – or from accompanying their performances with effeminate gestures and songs. Eminent women, too, rehearsed indecent parts. In the wood which Augustus had planted round his Naval Lake, places of assignation and taverns were built, and every stimulus to vice was displayed for sale. Moreover, there were distributions of money. Respectable people were compelled to spend it; disreputable people did so gladly. Promiscuity and degradation throve. Roman morals had long become impure, but never was there so favourable an environment for debauchery as among this filthy crowd. Even in good surroundings people find it hard to behave well. Here every form of immorality competed for attention, and no chastity, modesty, or vestige of decency could survive.

The climax was the emperor's stage debut. Meticulously tuning his lyre, he struck practice notes to the trainers beside him. A battalion attended with its officers. So did Burrus, grieving – but applauding. Now, too, was formed the corps of Roman knights known as the Augustiani. These powerful young men, impudent by nature or ambition, maintained a din of applause day and night, showering divine epithets on Nero's beauty and voice. They were grand and respected as if they had done great things.

But the emperor did not obtain publicity by his theatrical talents only. He also aspired to poetic taste. He gathered round himself at dinner men who possessed some versifying ability but were not yet known. As they sat on, they strung together verses they had brought with them, or extemporized – and filled out Nero's own suggestions, such as they were. This method is apparent from Nero's poems themselves, which lack vigour, inspiration, and homogeneity. To philosophers, too, he devoted some of his time after dinner, enjoying their quarrelsome assertions of contradictory views. There were enough of such people willing to display their glum features and expressions for the amusement of the court.

At about this time there was a serious fight between the inhabitants of two Roman settlements, Nuceria and Pompeii. It arose out of a trifling incident at a gladiatorial show given by Livineius Regulus (II), whose expulsion from the senate I have mentioned elsewhere. During an exchange of taunts – characteristic of these disorderly country towns – abuse led to stone-throwing, and then swords were drawn. The people of Pompeii, where the show was held, came off best. Many wounded and mutilated Nucerians were taken to the capital. Many bereavements, too, were suffered by parents and children. The emperor instructed the senate to investigate the affair. The senate passed it to the consuls. When they reported back, the senate debarred Pompeii from holding any similar gathering for ten years. Illegal associations in the town were dissolved; and the sponsor of the show and his fellow-instigators of the disorders were exiled.

Cyrene secured the expulsion of a governor, Pedius Blaesus, from the senate for violating their treasury of Aesculapius and accepting bribes and solicitations to falsify the recruiting rolls. Cyrene also prosecuted another ex-praetor, Acilius Strabo, who had been sent by Claudius to adjudicate on the ancestral royal estates which had been left, with the whole kingdom, to Rome by King Ptolemy Apion. Neighbouring landowners who had occupied these estates cited their longstanding usurpation as fair title. The adjudicator decided against them. So they reviled him. The senate answered that it did not know Claudius' instructions – reference must be made to the emperor. Nero upheld the adjudicator, but wrote that nevertheless he would help the provincial landowners by legalizing their occupation.

The deaths now occurred of two famous men, Cnaeus Domitius Afer and Marcus Servilius Nonianus (II). Both were great orators with distinguished records, Domitius as advocate, Servilius – after a long legal career – as Roman historian; also as man of taste, wherein he displayed a marked contrast with his otherwise equally brilliant rival.

In the following year, when Nero (for the fourth time) and Cossus Cornelius Lentulus (II) were consuls, a five-yearly stage-competition was founded at Rome on the Greek model. Like most innovations, its reception was mixed. Some recalled with approval the criticism of Pompey, among his elders, for constructing a permanent theatre, whereas previously performances had been held with improvised stage and auditorium, or (to go back to the remoter past) spectators had stood – since seats, it was feared, would keep them idle for days on end. 'As for the shows,' said objectors, 'let them continue in the old Roman way, whenever it falls to the praetors to celebrate them, and provided no citizen is obliged to compete. Traditional morals, already gradually deteriorating, have been utterly ruined by this imported laxity! It makes everything potentially corrupting and corruptible flow into the capital – foreign influences demoralize our young men into shirkers, gymnasts, and perverts.

'Responsibility rests with emperor and senate. They have given immorality a free hand. Now they are compelling the Roman upper class to degrade themselves as orators or singers on the stage. It only remains to strip and fight in boxing-gloves instead of joining the army. Does expert attention to effeminate music and songs contribute to justice, or does it make the knights who serve as judges give better verdicts? And this vileness continues even at night! Good behaviour has no time left for it. In these promiscuous crowds, debauchees are emboldened to practise by night the lusts they have imagined by day.'

This licence was just what most people approved – though they put it more respectably. 'But our ancestors, too,' they suggested, 'did not shrink from such public entertainment as contemporary resources permitted. Ballet-dancers were imported from Etruria, horse-racing from Thurii. Ever since the annexation of Greece and Asia performances have become more ambitious. Two hundred years have passed since the Triumph of Lucius

Mummius – who first gave that sort of show here – and during that time no upper-class Roman has ever demeaned himself by *professional* acting. As for a permanent theatre, it was more economical than the construction and demolition of a new one every year, at vast expense.

'If – as now suggested – the State pays for shows, it will save the purses of officials and give the public less opportunity to ask them for Greek contests. Prizes for oratory and poetry will encourage talent. And why should it be degrading even for a judge to listen with legitimate enjoyment to fine words? These nights – not many, out of a period of five years – are for gaiety, not immorality. Besides, in such a blaze of lights, surreptitious immorality is impossible.'

Certainly, the display took place without any open scandal. Nor was there any partisan rioting, since the ballet-dancers, though allowed back on the stage, were banned from these sacred contests. The first prize for oratory was not awarded, but the emperor was declared winner. Greek clothes, which had been greatly worn during the competition, subsequently went out of fashion.

A brilliant comet now appeared. The general belief is that a comet means a change of emperor. So people speculated on Nero's successor as though Nero were already dethroned. Everybody talked of Rubellius Plautus, a Julian on his mother's side. His personal tastes were old-fashioned, his bearing austere, and his life respectable and secluded. Retirement, due to fear, had enhanced his reputation. The talk about the comet was intensified by equally superstitious reactions to a flash of lightning, which struck and broke the table at which Nero was dining in his mansion at Sublaqueum near the Simbruine Lakes. Since this was near Tibur, the birthplace of Plautus' father, the belief arose that the Divine Will had marked Plautus out. He was frequently courted by those whose devouring and often misguided ambitions attach them prematurely to new and hazardous causes. Nero was worried. He wrote asking Plautus, in the interests of the city's peace, to withdraw from malevolent gossip to enjoy his youthful years in the safety and calm of his family estates in Asia. So there Plautus went, with his wife, Antistia Pollitta, and his closest friends.

Nero, in these days, endangered and discredited himself by an extravagent eccentricity: he bathed in the source of the Marcian Aqueduct. His immersion therein was held to have polluted the sanctity of its holy waters. The divine anger was apparent when he became seriously ill.

[. . .]

The same year witnessed two noteworthy crimes at Rome. One of the audacious perpetrators was a senator, the other a slave. Domitius Balbus was a former praetor whose age, wealth, and childlessness exposed him to fraudulence. His relative Valerius Fabianus (a man destined for an official career) forged Domitius' will. Two knights, Vinicius Rufinus and Terentius Lentinus, who were Valerius' accomplices, brought in Marcus Antonius

Primus, a man ready for anything, and Marcus Asinius Marcellus, who had the distinction of being the great-grandson of Gaius Asinius Pollio (I) and was respected – apart from his belief that poverty was the supreme misfortune. So with these associates, and others of less account, Valerius sealed the document. When this was proved in the senate, the forgers were all convicted under the Cornelian law against falsification, except Marcellus, who escaped punishment owing to the emperor's intervention in memory of his ancestors. Disgrace he did not escape.

On the same day a young ex-quaestor, Pompeius Aelianus, was condemned for complicity in the same crime and banned from Italy and his home country, Spain. Valerius Ponticus was excluded from Italy for conducting prosecutions before the praetor to avoid trial by the City Prefect – a procedure which, while preserving legality for the time being, aimed at ultimate acquittal by collusion. A clause was added to the relevant senatorial decree making anyone who bought or sold such conniv-ance liable to the same penalty as if convicted by false accusation in a criminal case.

Soon afterwards the City Prefect, Lucius Pedanius Secundus, was murdered by one of his slaves. Either Pedanius had refused to free the murderer after agreeing to a price, or the slave, infatuated with some man or other, found competition from his master intolerable. After the murder, ancient custom required that every slave residing under the same roof must be executed. But a crowd gathered, eager to save so many innocent lives; and rioting began. The senate-house was besieged.

Inside, there was feeling against excessive severity, but the majority opposed any change. Among the latter was Gaius Cassius Longinus, who when his turn came spoke as follows:

'I have often been here, senators, when decrees deviating from our ancestral laws and customs were mooted. I have not opposed them. Not that I had any doubts about the superiority – in every matter whatsoever – of ancient arrangements, and the undesirability of every change. But I did not wish, by exaggerated regard for antique usage, to show too high an opinion of my own profession, the law. Nor did I want, by continual opposition, to weaken any influence I may possess. I wanted to keep it intact in case the country needed my advice.

'It needs it today! A man who has held the consulship has been deliberately murdered by a slave in his own home. None of his fellow-slaves prevented or betrayed the murderer, though the senatorial decree threatening the whole household with execution still stands. Exempt them from the penalty if you like. But then, if the City Prefect was not important enough to be immune, who will be? Who will have enough slaves to protect him if Pedanius' four hundred were too few? Who can rely on his household's help if even fear for their own lives does not make them shield us?

'Or was the assassin avenging a wrong? For that is one shameless fabrication. Tell us next that the slave had been negotiating about his patrimony, or he had lost some ancestral property! We had better call it justifiable homicide straightaway.

'When wiser men have in past times considered and settled the whole matter, will you dare to refute them? Pretend, if you like, that we are deciding a policy for the first time. Do you believe that a slave can have planned to kill his master without letting fall a single rash or menacing word? Or even if we assume he kept his secret – and obtained a weapon unnoticed – could he have passed the watch, opened the bedroom door, carried in a light, and committed the murder, without any-one knowing? There are many advance notifications of crimes. If slaves give them away, we can live securely, though one among many, because of their insecurity; or, if we must die, we can at least be sure the guilty will be punished.

'Our ancestors distrusted their slaves. Yet slaves were then born on the same estates, in the same homes, as their masters, who had treated them kindly from birth. But nowadays our huge households are international. They include every alien religion – or none at all. The only way to keep down this scum is by intimidation. Innocent people will die, you say. Yes, and when in a defeated army every tenth man is flogged to death, the brave have to draw lots with the others. Exemplary punishment always contains an element of injustice. But individual wrongs are outweighed by the advantage of the community.'

No one dared speak up against Cassius. But there were protesting cries of pity for the numbers affected, and the women, and the young, and the undoubted innocence of the majority. Yet those favouring execution prevailed. However, great crowds ready with stones and torches prevented the order from being carried out. Nero rebuked the population by edict, and lined with troops the whole route along which those condemned were taken for execution. Then it was proposed by Cingonius Varro that the ex-slaves, too, who had been under the same roof should be deported from Italy. But the emperor vetoed this – the ancient custom had not been tempered by mercy, but should not be aggravated by brutality.

Bithynia, this year, secured the condemnation of its governor, Tarquitius Priscus, for extortion. The senate, remembering that he had once accused his own governor, Titus Statilius Taurus (II), was delighted. In Gaul, a census was carried out by Quintus Volusius Saturninus, Titus Sextius Africanus, and Lucius Trebellius Maximus. The aristocratic Volusius and Sextius were rivals, and both despised Trebellius, who took advantage of their bickering to get the better of them.

Publius Memmius Regulus now died. His influence, dignity and good name had attained the greatest glory which the all-overshadowing imperial grandeur permits. Indeed, when Nero was ill, and sycophantic courtiers declared that his death would mean the end of the empire, the emperor answered that the State had a support; and when they asked what he meant, he replied: 'Memmius Regulus.' Yet Regulus survived unharmed. For he was inactive, his family was only recently ennobled, and his resources were too insignificant to attract envy.

Another event of this year was the dedication of a gymnasium by Nero. Oil was distributed to senators and knights on a truly Greek scale of extravagance. In the following year, when the consuls were Publius Marius Celsus and Lucius Afinius Gallus, the praetor Antistius Sosianus, whose disorderly behaviour as tribune I have mentioned, wrote verses satirizing the emperor, and read them aloud at a large dinner-party given by Marcus Ostorius Scapula. Antistius was charged with treason by Cossutianus Capito, who on the entreaty of his father-in-law Gaius Ofonius Tigellinus had recently been made a senator. This was the first revival of the treason law. The intention – people believed – was not so much to ruin Antistius as to enable the emperor to gain credit by using his tribune's authority to veto the senate's adverse verdict.

The host testified that he had heard nothing. Yet contrary witnesses were believed, and one of the consuls-designate, Quintus Junius Marullus, moved Antistius' deposition from the praetorship, to be followed by execution in the ancient manner. There was general agreement. But Thrasea, after highly complimenting Nero and vigorously blaming Antistius, argued that under so excellent an emperor the senate was liable to no compulsion, and need not inflict the maximum punishment deserved. The executioner and the noose were obsolete, said Thrasea; the laws had extablished penalties which exempted judges from brutality and avoided undesirable anachronisms; so let Antistius have his property confiscated and be sent to an island, where every prolongation of his guilty life would intensify his personal misery but splendidly illustrate official mercy.

Thrasea's independence made others less servile. So

his proposal, when the consul put the vote, was carried. Among the few dissentients the worst sycophant was Aulus Vitellius.* Like other cowards he insulted anyone decent, but kept quiet when answered back. However, the consuls did not venture to confirm the senate's decree, but wrote informing Nero of the general view. Anger and discretion fought within him. Finally he sent the following reply: 'Antistius, unprovoked, has grossly abused the emperor. The senate was asked to punish him. It ought to have fixed a punishment fitting the enormity of the crime. But I will not amend your leniency. Indeed, I should not have allowed anything else. Decide as you please. You could have acquitted him if you wished.'

These and similar comments were read out. Nero was clearly offended. Yet the consuls did not change the motion. Thrasea did not alter his proposal, and the others, too, adhered to their decision. Some wanted to avoid showing the emperor in an unfavourable light. The majority saw safety in numbers. Thrasea was showing his usual resolution – and conformity with his reputation.

Aulus Didius Gallus Fabricius Veiento fell to a similar charge, namely the inclusion in a so-called will of numerous insults against senators and priests. His accuser, Gaius Terentius Tullius Geminus, added that Veiento had accepted bribery, in return for his influence with the emperor regarding official promotions. This led Nero to deal with the case himself. He found Veiento guilty, expelled him from Italy, and ordered his writings to be

* This is the future emperor Vitellius (AD 69).

burnt. These were eagerly sought for and read – while it was dangerous to have them. When, later, the ban became obsolete, they were forgotten.

The situation of the country was deteriorating every day; and a counteracting influence now vanished, with the death of Burrus. Whether natural causes or poison killed him is uncertain. The gradually increasing tumour in his throat, which blocked the passage and stopped his breathing, suggested natural causes. But the general view was that Nero, ostensibly proposing a medical treatment, had instructed that Burrus' throat should be painted with a poisonous drug. The patient, it was said, had detected the crime, and when the emperor visited him had turned his face away and only answered Nero's inquiries with the words: '*I* am doing all right.'

The death of Burrus caused great public distress. His merits were dwelt on – also the inferiority of his successors, one harmless but ineffective and the other a notorious criminal. For the emperor now appointed two commanders of the Guard – Faenius Rufus because he was popular (having managed the corn supply without personal profit), and Gaius Ofonius Tigellinus because Nero found his unending immoralities and evil reputation fascinating. Each commander behaved as expected. Tigellinus was the more influential with the emperor, in whose private debaucheries he participated. Rufus was liked by Guardsmen and civilians: which went against him with Nero.

Burrus' death undermined the influence of Seneca. Decent standards carried less weight when one of their two advocates was gone. Now Nero listened to more disreputable advisers. These attacked Seneca, first for his wealth, which was enormous and excessive for any subject, they said, and was still increasing; secondly, for the grandeur of his mansions and beauty of his gardens, which outdid even the emperor's; and thirdly, for his alleged bids for popularity. They also charged Seneca with allowing no one to be called eloquent but himself. 'He is always writing poetry,' they suggested, 'now that Nero has become fond of it. He openly disparages the emperor's amusements, underestimates him as a charioteer, and makes fun of his singing. How long must merit at Rome be conferred by Seneca's certificate alone? Surely Nero is a boy no longer! He is a grown man and ought to discharge his tutor. His ancestors will teach him all he needs.' Seneca knew of these attacks. People who still had some decency told him of them. Nero increasingly avoided his company.

Seneca, however, requested an audience, and when it was granted, this is what he said. 'It is nearly fourteen years, Caesar, since I became associated with your rising fortunes, eight since you became emperor. During that time you have showered on me such distinctions and riches that, if only I could retire to enjoy them unpretentiously, my prosperity would be complete.

'May I quote illustrious precedents drawn from your rank, not mine? Your great-great-grandfather Augustus allowed Marcus Agrippa to withdraw to Mytilene, and allowed Gaius Maecenas the equivalent of retirement at Rome itself. The one his partner in wars, the other the bearer of many anxious burdens at Rome, they were greatly rewarded, for great services. I have had no claim on your generosity, except my learning. Though acquired outside the glare of public life, it has brought me the wonderful recompense and distinction of having assisted in your early education.

'But you have also bestowed on me measureless favours, and boundless wealth. Accordingly, I often ask myself: "Is it I, son of a provincial knight, who am accounted a national leader? Is mine the unknown name which has come to glitter among ancient and glorious pedigrees? Where is my old self, that was content with so little? Laying out these fine gardens? Grandly inspecting these estates? Wallowing in my vast revenues?" I can only find one excuse. It was not for me to obstruct your munificence.

'But we have both filled the measure – you, of what an emperor can give his friend, and I, of what a friend may receive from his emperor. Anything more will breed envy. Your greatness is far above all such mortal things. But I am not; so I crave your help. If, in the field or on a journey, I were tired, I should want a stick. In life's journey, I need just such a support.

'For I am old and cannot do the lightest work. I am no longer equal to the burden of my wealth. Order your agents to take over my property and incorporate it in yours. I do not suggest plunging myself into poverty, but giving up the things that are too brilliant and dazzle me. The time now spent on gardens and mansions shall be devoted to the mind. You have abundant strength. For years the supreme power has been familiar to you. We older friends may ask for our rest. This, too, will add to your glory – that you have raised to the heights men content with lower positions.'

The substance of Nero's reply was this. 'My first debt to you is that I can reply impromptu to your premeditated speech. For you taught me to improvise as well as to make prepared orations. True, my great-great-grandfather Augustus permitted Agrippa and Maecenas to rest after their labours. But he did so when he was old enough to assure them, by his prestige, of everything – of whatever kind – that he had given them. Besides, he certainly deprived neither of the rewards which they had earned from him in the wars and crises of Augustus' youthful years. If my life had been warlike, you too would have fought for me. But you gave what our situation demanded: wisdom, advice, philosophy, to support me as boy and youth. Your gifts to me will endure as long as life itself! My gifts to you, gardens and mansions and revenues, are liable to circumstances.

'They may seem extensive. But many people far less deserving than you have had more. I omit, from shame, to mention ex-slaves who flaunt greater wealth. I am even ashamed that you, my dearest friend, are not the richest of all men. You are still vigorous and fit for State affairs and their rewards. My reign is only beginning. Or do you think you have reached your limit? If so you must rank yourself below Lucius Vitellius, thrice consul, and my generosity below that of Claudius, and my gifts as inferior to the lifelong savings of Lucius Volusius Saturninus (II).

'If youth's slippery paths lead me astray, be at hand to

call me back! You equipped my manhood; devote even greater care to guiding it! If you return my gifts and desert your emperor, it is not your unpretentiousness, your retirement, that will be on everyone's lips, but *my* meanness, your dread of *my* brutality. However much your self-denial were praised, no philosopher could becomingly gain credit from an action damaging to his friend's reputation.'

Then he clasped and kissed Seneca. Nature and experience had fitted Nero to conceal hatred behind treacherous embraces. Seneca expressed his gratitude (all conversations with autocrats end like that). But he abandoned the customs of his former ascendancy. Terminating his large receptions, he dismissed his entourage, and rarely visited Rome. Ill-health or philosophical studies kept him at home, he said.

After Seneca's elimination it was easy to bring down the commander of the Guard Faenius Rufus, who was accused of friendship with Agrippina. Faenius' colleague Tigellinus became more powerful every day. But he felt that his criminal aptitudes – the only qualities he possessed – would influence the emperor more if he could make them partners in crime. Studying Nero's fears, Tigellinus found he chiefly dreaded Rubellius Plautus and Faustus Cornelius Sulla Felix. One had been recently removed to Asia, the other to southern Gaul. Tigellinus enlarged on their aristocratic origins, and their present proximity to the armies of the east and of Germany respectively.

'I have no divided allegiance like Burrus,' he said. 'My only thought is your safety! At Rome this may in some degree be ensured by vigilance on the spot. But how can one suppress sedition far away? The dictator Sulla's name has excited the Gauls. For the peoples of Asia Drusus' grandson is just as unsettling. Sulla's poverty increases his daring. He pretends to be lazy – yet he is only biding his time for a *coup*. Plautus is rich, and does not pretend to like retirement. He parades an admiration of the ancient Romans, but he has the arrogance of the Stoics, who breed sedition and intrigue.'

Action was not long delayed. Five days later, Sulla was murdered at dinner. Assassins had reached Massilia before the alarm. His head was transported to Nero, who joked that it was disfigured by premature greyness.

The plans for Plautus' death were less secret. More people were interested in his safety. Besides, the length and duration of the land and sea journeys encouraged rumours. The story was invented that Plautus had escaped to Corbulo who, having mighty armies behind him, would be in the gravest peril if there was to be a massacre of blameless notables. Asia, it was said, had risen in Plautus' support; the few, unenthusiastic, soldiers sent to murder him had failed to carry out their orders and had joined the rebellion. Idle credulity, as usual, amplified these fictitious rumours.

Meanwhile an ex-slave of Plautus, helped by favourable winds, outstripped the staff-officer of the Guard who had been sent against him, and brought a message from Plautus' father-in-law Lucius Antistius Vetus. 'Escape a passive end while there is a way out!' advised Antistius. 'Sympathy for your great name will make decent men back you and brave men help you. Meantime, disdain no possible support. Sixty soldiers have been sent. If you can repulse them, much can happen – even a war can develop – before Nero receives the news and sends another force. In short, either you save yourself by this action, or at least a bold end is as good as a timid one.'

But Plautus remained unimpressed. Either he felt helpless – an unarmed exile – or the suspense wearied him. Or perhaps he believed that his wife and children, whom he loved, would be more leniently treated if the emperor were not upset by an alarm. One account states that his father-in-law sent further messages saying that Plautus was in no danger. Or his philosophical friends, the Greek Coeranus and the Etruscan Gaius Musonius Rufus, may have recommended an imperturbable expectation of death rather than a hazardous anxious life.

The killers found him at midday, stripped for exercise. Supervised by the eunuch Pelago whom Nero had put in charge of the gang – like a slave set over a monarch's underlings – the officer slew him as he was. The victim's head was brought to Nero. I will quote the actual words he uttered when he saw it. 'Nero,' he said, 'how could such a long-nosed man have frightened you?'

Indeed, the fears which had caused the emperor to postpone his wedding with Poppaea were now dispelled. He planned to marry her quickly, after eliminating Octavia his wife. Octavia's conduct was unassuming; but he hated her, because she was popular and an emperor's daughter. First Nero wrote to the senate emphasizing his perpetual solicitude for the national interests, and – without admitting their murder – denouncing Sulla and Plautus as agitators. On these grounds the senate voted a thanksgiving, and the two men's expulsion from the senate. This was a mockery which caused greater disgust even than the crimes. Hearing of their decree, Nero concluded that all his misdeeds were accounted meritorious. So he divorced Octavia for barrenness, and married Poppaea.

Dominating Nero as his wife, as she had long dominated him as his mistress, Poppaea incited one of Octavia's household to accuse Octavia of adultery with a slave – an Alexandrian flute-player called Eucaerus was designated for the role. Octavia's maids were tortured, and though some were induced by the pain to make false confessions, the majority unflinchingly maintained her innocence. One retorted that the mouth of Tigellinus, who was bullying her, was less clean than any part of Octavia. Nevertheless, she was put away. First, there was an ordinary divorce: she received the ominous gifts of Burrus' house and Rubellius Plautus' estates. Soon, however, she was banished to Campania, under military surveillance.

Now indiscretion is safer for the Roman public than for their superiors, since they are insignificant; and they protested openly and loudly. This seemed to recall Nero to decency, and he proposed to make Octavia his wife again. Happy crowds climbed the Capitol, thankful to heaven at last. They overturned Poppaea's statues and carried Octavia's on their shoulders, showering flowers on them and setting them in the Forum and temples.

Even the emperor was acclaimed and worshipped again. Indeed a noisy crowd invaded the palace. But detachments of troops clubbed them and forced them back at the point of the sword. Then the changes the rioters had inspired were reversed, and Poppaea reinstated. Always a savage hater, she was now mad with fear of mass violence and Nero's capitulation to it. She fell at his feet crying: 'Now that things have reached this pass, it is not marriage I am fighting for, but what, to me, means less than my marriage – my life. It is in danger from Octavia's dependants and slaves! They pretend to be the people of Rome! They commit, in peace-time, outrages that could hardly happen even in war! The emperor is their target – they only lack a leader. And once disorders begin one will easily be found, when she leaves Campania and proceeds to the capital! Even her distant nod causes riots.

'What have *I* done wrong? Whom have I injured? Or is all this because I am going to give an authentic heir to the house of the Caesars? Would Rome prefer an Egyptian flute-player's child to be introduced into the palace? If you think it best, take back your directress voluntarily – do not be coerced into doing so. Or else, safeguard yourself! Punish suitably. No severity was needed to end the first troubles. But now, once they lose hope of Nero keeping Octavia, they will find her another husband.'

Poppaea's arguments, playing on Nero's alarm and anger in turn, duly terrified and infuriated him. But the suspicions concerning Octavia's slave came to nothing; the examination of her servants proved fruitless. So it was decided to extract a confession of adultery from someone against whom a charge of revolution could also be concocted. A suitable person seemed to be the aforementioned Anicetus, fleet-commander at Misenum and instrument of Nero's matricide. After the crime he had been fairly well regarded. Later, however, he was in serious disfavour; for the sight of a former accomplice in terrible crimes is a reproach.

Nero summoned him, and reminded him of his previous job – Anicetus alone had protected his emperor against his mother's plotting. Now, said Nero, he could earn equal gratitude by eliminating a detested wife. No violence or weapons were needed. Anicetus only had to confess adultery with Octavia. Great rewards were promised – though at present they were unspecified – and an agreed place of retirement. Refusal would mean death. Anicetus' warped character found no difficulty in a further crime. Indeed, the confession which he made to Nero's friends, assembled as a council of state, even exceeded his instructions. Then he was removed to comfortable exile in Sardinia, where he died a natural death.

Nero reported in an edict that Octavia had tried to win over the fleet by seducing its commander, and then, nervous about her unfaithfulness, had procured an abortion (the emperor forgot his recent charge of sterility). She was then confined on the island of Pandateria.

No exiled woman ever earned greater sympathy from those who saw her. Some still remembered the banishment of the elder Agrippina by Tiberius and, more recently, of Julia Livilla by Claudius. Yet they had been mature women with happy memories which could alleviate their present sufferings. But Octavia had virtually died on her wedding day. Her new home had brought her nothing but misery. Poison had removed her father, and very soon her brother. Maid had been preferred to mistress. Then she, Nero's wife, had been ruined by her successor. Last came the bitterest of all fates, this accusation.

So this girl, in her twentieth year, was picketed by company-commanders of the Guard and their men. She was hardly a living person any more – so certain was she of imminent destruction. Yet still she lacked the peace of death. The order to die arrived a few days later. She protested that she was a wife no longer – Nero's sister only. She invoked the Germanici, the relations she shared with Nero. Finally she even invoked Agrippina, in whose days her marriage had been unhappy, certainly, but at least not fatal. But Octavia was bound, and all her veins were opened. However, her terror retarded the flow of blood. So she was put into an exceedingly hot vapour-bath and suffocated. An even crueller atrocity followed. Her head was cut off and taken to Rome for Poppaea to see.

How long must I go on recording the thank-offerings in temples on such occasions? Every reader about that epoch, in my own work or others, can assume that the gods were thanked every time the emperor ordered a banishment or murder; and, conversely, that happenings once regarded joyfully were now treated as national disasters. Nevertheless, when any senatorial decree reaches new depths of sycophancy or abasement, I will not leave it unrecorded.

In the same year Nero was believed to have poisoned two of his most prominent ex-slaves – Doryphorus for opposing the emperor's marriage with Poppaea, and Pallas for reserving his own immense riches for himself by living so long.

Seneca was secretly denounced by Romanus as an associate of Gaius Calpurnius Piso. But Seneca more effectively turned the same charge against his accuser. However, the incident alarmed Piso – and by so doing initiated a far-reaching, disastrous conspiracy against Nero.

The Burning of Rome

As a further distraction from the grave foreign situation, certain corn that had been intended for the inhabitants of Rome but had deteriorated in storage was dumped by Nero in the Tiber. This was to inspire confidence that supplies were abundant. However, nearly two hundred corn-ships – actually in harbour – had been destroyed by a violent storm, and a hundred more were accidentally burnt when already up the Tiber. Yet the emperor did not increase the price. But he proceeded to appoint three ex-consuls, Lucius Calpurnius Piso (V), Aulus Ducenius Geminus, and Pompeius Paulinus, to control the national revenues. Nero utilized this occasion to criticize previous emperors for their ruinous expenditure in advance of income, and to emphasize his own annual gifts of sixty million sesterces to the nation.

At this period there was a widespread harmful practice whereby, when an election or ballot for governorships was impending, childless persons fictitiously adopted sons, and then, when they had won praetorships or provinces as fathers of families, immediately emancipated the adopted persons. The senate received angry appeals from real parents. These contrasted the unnatural, fraudulent brevity of these adoptions with the natural claims of themselves, who had suffered the anxieties of bringing up children. The childless were amply consoled, they argued, by the ready ease with which, carefree and unburdened, they acquired influence and office; whereas their own legal privileges, after protracted waiting, became a farce when some irresponsible so-called father – whose lack of children did not come from bereavement – effortlessly achieved the longstanding ambitions of authentic parents. So the senate decreed that, when offices or even inheritances were at stake, fictitious adoptions should carry no weight.

Next came the trial of a Cretan, Claudius Timarchus. Most of the charges against him were those habitually brought against mighty provincials whose enormous wealth inflates them into oppressors. But he had also made a remark (more than once) which constituted an insult to the senate: 'Whether a governor of Crete receives the thanks of our Provincial Assembly depends on me!' Thrasea utilized the occasion to the national advantage. Proposing the defendant's banishment from Crete, he reminded the senate how experience showed that, among right-thinking men, good laws and beneficial precedents are prompted by other men's misdeeds. Punishments, he pointed out, come after crimes, and rectifications after abuses. He quoted the Cincian bill originating from the excesses of advocates, the Julian laws from corruption among candidates, and the Calpurnian enactments from the rapacity of officials.

'So let us face this unprecedented provincial arrogance,' he urged, 'with a measure befitting Roman honour and dignity. Without diminishing our protection of provincials, we must recover the conviction that a Roman's reputation depends on Romans only. Once we used to send praetors and consuls, and even private citizens, to inspect provinces and report on everyone's loyalty. Then nations trembled for the verdict of one man! But now we court and flatter foreigners. Some individual makes a sign, and they thank our governor – or, more likely, prosecute him!

'But even granting that we must continue to let provincials display their power in this way, we should nevertheless frown on governors winning empty eulogies, extracted by entreaties. We should judge this as severely as ill-intentioned or brutal government. To oblige is often as harmful as to offend. Indeed, some virtues provoke hatred. Unbending strictness and incorruptibility do. That is why our officials usually start well and end badly; like election candidates, they begin looking round for support. Stop this, and provincial administration will be fairer and steadier. Prohibit votes of thanks, and popularity-hunting will collapse – just as acquisitiveness is repressed by fear of the extortion laws.'

These opinions received warm approval. But no senatorial decree could be carried, since the consuls ruled that no question on the subject was before the House. Later, however, on the emperor's initiative, a decree was passed forbidding votes of thanks to governors at Provincial Assemblies, or the participation by provincials in missions conveying such votes.

This, too, was the year in which the Gymnasium was struck by lightning and burnt down. A statue of Nero inside was melted into a shapeless bronze mass. An earthquake also largely demolished the populous

Campanian town of Pompeii. Laelia, priestess of Vesta, died, and her place was taken by Cornelia, of the family of the Cossi.

Next year the consuls were Gaius Memmius Regulus and Lucius Verginius Rufus. Poppaea now bore Nero a daughter. His joy exceeded human measure, and mother and child were both named Augusta. The infant was born at Nero's own birthplace, the Roman settlement of Antium. The senate had already asked heaven's blessing on Poppaea's pregnancy and made official vows. Now these vows were discharged, with additions including a thanksgiving. A temple of Fertility was decreed, and a competition modelled on the Actian Victory Festival. Golden statues of the Two Fortunes of Antium were to be placed on the throne of Capitoline Jupiter, and Antium was to have Circus Games in honour of the Claudian and Domitian houses, like the Games in honour of the Julian house at Bovillae.

But it was all ephemeral; for within less than four months the baby was dead. Then followed new forms of sycophancy. She was declared a goddess and voted a place on the gods' ceremonial couch, together with a shrine and a priest. The emperor's delight had been immoderate; so was his mourning.

Shortly after the birth, the whole senate had flocked out to Antium. But Thrasea had been forbidden to attend. It was noticed how calmly he received this affront – though it foreshadowed his own impending death. Nero, it is said, subsequently boasted to Seneca that he was reconciled with Thrasea; and Seneca congratulated

Nero. The incident increased both these eminent men's prestige, but also their peril.

[...]

Other events of this year were the award of Latin rights to the tribes of the Maritime Alps, and the allocation to Roman knights of places in the Circus in front of the ordinary people's seats. Hitherto the order of knights had possessed no separate seats in the Circus because the Roscian law allotting them 'the first fourteen rows' applied only to the theatre.

[...]

The same year witnessed gladiatorial displays on a no less magnificent scale than before, but exceeding all precedent in the number of distinguished women and senators disgracing themselves in the arena. When the new year began, with Gaius Laecanius Bassus and Marcus Licinius Crassus Frugi (II) as consuls, Nero showed daily-increasing impatience to appear regularly on the public stage. Hitherto, he had sung at home, or at the Youth Games held in his Gardens. But he began to disdain such occasions as insufficiently attended and too restricted for a voice like his. Not venturing, however, to make his début at Rome, he selected Neapolis, as being a Greek city. Starting there, he planned to cross to Greece, win the glorious and long-revered wreaths of its Games, and thus increase his fame and popularity at home.

The Neapolitan theatre was filled. Besides the local population, it contained visitors from all around attracted by the notable occasion. Present, too, were those who attend the emperor out of respect or to perform various services – and even units of troops. The theatre now provided what seemed to most people an evil omen, but to Nero a sign of divine providence and favour. For when it was empty (the crowd having left), it collapsed. But there were no casualties; and Nero composed a poem thanking the gods for the happy outcome of the incident.

Then, on his way to cross the Adriatic, he stopped for a while at Beneventum. There large crowds were attending a gladiatorial display given by a certain Vatinius. This outstanding monstrosity of the court had originated from a shoe shop. Deformed in body and scurrilous in wit, he had first been taken up as a butt for abuse. But then he gained power enough to eclipse any scoundrel in influence, wealth, and capacity for damage. He rose by attacking decent people.

But even at his pleasures, attending this man's show, Nero took no vacation from crime. For enforced death now came to Decimus Junius Silanus Torquatus. This was because, in addition to the nobility of his Junian house, he could claim the divine Augustus as a great-great-grandfather. The accusers were instructed to charge Torquatus with generosity so extravagant that revolution had become his only hope. Censure was also to be directed against the titles which he gave some of his former slaves – Secretary-General, Petitions Secretary, and Financial Secretary. These, it was alleged, were titles of an imperial household: Torquatus must be preparing for one. His confidential ex-slaves were arrested and removed. Seeing conviction ahead, he opened his veins. Nero made the usual pronouncement indicating that, however guilty and rightly distrustful of his defence Torquatus had been, he would nevertheless – if he had awaited his judge's mercy – have lived.

Before long Nero, for some reason unknown, postponed his visit to Greece, and returned to Rome. But he still planned to visit the eastern provinces, particularly Egypt; and his secret thoughts dwelt on them. After announcing by edict that his absence would be brief and all branches of government would carry on with undiminished efficiency, he proceeded to the Capitol for consultation about his journey. After worshipping the Capitoline gods, he entered the shrine of Vesta. But there all his limbs suddenly began to tremble. The goddess frightened him. Or perhaps he was always frightened, remembering his crimes. At all events, he abandoned this journey too.

His patriotism came before everything, Nero asserted; he had seen the people's sad faces and heard their private lamentations about the extensive travels he planned – even his brief absences they found unendurable, being accustomed (he added) to derive comfort in life's misfortunes from the sight of their emperor. Just as in private relationships nearest are dearest, he said, so to him the inhabitants of Rome came first: he must obey their appeal to stay! The people liked such protestations. They loved their amusements. But their principal interest was the corn supply: and they feared it would run short if

Nero went away. Senators and leading men were uncertain whether he was more abominable present or absent. Subsequently, as happens when men undergo terrifying experiences, the alternative that had befallen them seemed the graver.

Nero himself now tried to make it appear that Rome was his favourite abode. He gave feasts in public places as if the whole city were his own home. But the most prodigal and notorious banquet was given by Tigellinus. To avoid repetitious accounts of extravagance, I shall describe it, as a model of its kind. The entertainment took place on a raft constructed on Marcus Agrippa's lake. It was towed about by other vessels, with gold and ivory fittings. Their rowers were degenerates, assorted according to age and vice. Tigellinus had also collected birds and animals from remote countries, and even the products of the ocean. On the quays were brothels stocked with high-ranking ladies. Opposite them could be seen naked prostitutes, indecently posturing and gesturing.

At nightfall the woods and houses nearby echoed with singing and blazed with lights. Nero was already corrupted by every lust, natural and unnatural. But he now refuted any surmises that no further degradation was possible for him. For a few days later he went through a formal wedding ceremony with one of the perverted gang called Pythagoras. The emperor, in the presence of witnesses, put on the bridal veil. Dowry, marriage bed, wedding torches, all were there. Indeed everything was public which even in a natural union is veiled by night.

*

Disaster followed. Whether it was accidental or caused by a criminal act on the part of the emperor is uncertain – both versions have supporters. Now started the most terrible and destructive fire which Rome had ever experienced. It began in the Circus, where it adjoins the Palatine and Caelian hills. Breaking out in shops selling inflammable goods, and fanned by the wind, the conflagration instantly grew and swept the whole length of the Circus. There were no walled mansions or temples, or any other obstructions, which could arrest it. First, the fire swept violently over the level spaces. Then it climbed the hills – but returned to ravage the lower ground again. It outstripped every counter-measure. The ancient city's narrow winding streets and irregular blocks encouraged its progress.

Terrified, shrieking women, helpless old and young, people intent on their own safety, people unselfishly supporting invalids or waiting for them, fugitives and lingerers alike – all heightened the confusion. When people looked back, menacing flames sprang up before them or outflanked them. When they escaped to a neighbouring quarter, the fire followed – even districts believed remote proved to be involved. Finally, with no idea where or what to flee, they crowded on to the country roads, or lay in the fields. Some who had lost everything – even their food for the day – could have escaped, but preferred to die. So did others, who had failed to rescue their loved ones. Nobody dared fight the flames. Attempts to do so were prevented by menacing gangs. Torches, too, were openly thrown in, by men crying that they acted under orders. Perhaps they had received orders. Or they may just have wanted to plunder unhampered.

Nero was at Antium. He only returned to the city when the fire was approaching the mansion he had built to link the Gardens of Maecenas to the Palatine. The flames could not be prevented from overwhelming the whole of the Palatine, including his palace. Nevertheless, for the relief of the homeless, fugitive masses he threw open the Field of Mars, including Agrippa's public buildings, and even his own Gardens. Nero also constructed emergency accommodation for the destitute multitude. Food was brought from Ostia and neighbouring towns, and the price of corn was cut to less than ¼ sesterce a pound. Yet these measures, for all their popular character, earned no gratitude. For a rumour had spread that, while the city was burning, Nero had gone on his private stage and, comparing modern calamities with ancient, had sung of the destruction of Troy.

By the sixth day enormous demolitions had confronted the raging flames with bare ground and open sky, and the fire was finally stamped out at the foot of the Esquiline Hill. But before panic had subsided, or hope revived, flames broke out again in the more open regions of the city. Here there were fewer casualties; but the destruction of temples and pleasure arcades was even worse. This new conflagration caused additional ill-feeling because it started on Tigellinus' estate in the Aemilian district. For people believed that Nero was ambitious to found a new city to be called after himself.

Of Rome's fourteen districts only four remained intact. Three were levelled to the ground. The other seven were reduced to a few scorched and mangled ruins. To count the mansions, blocks, and temples destroyed would be difficult. They included shrines of remote antiquity, such as Servius Tullius' temple of the Moon, the Great Altar and holy place dedicated by Evander to Hercules, the temple vowed by Romulus to Jupiter the Stayer, Numa's sacred residence, and Vesta's shrine containing Rome's household gods. Among the losses, too, were the precious spoils of countless victories, Greek artistic masterpieces, and authentic records of old Roman genius. All the splendour of the rebuilt city did not prevent the older generation from remembering these irreplaceable objects. It was noted that the fire had started on July 19th, the day on which the Senonian Gauls had captured and burnt the city. Others elaborately calculated that the two fires were separated by the same number of years, months, and days.*

But Nero profited by his country's ruin to build a new palace. Its wonders were not so much customary and commonplace luxuries like gold and jewels, but lawns and lakes and faked rusticity – woods here, open spaces and views there. With their cunning, impudent artificialities, Nero's architects and engineers, Severus and Celer, did not balk at effects which Nature herself had ruled out as impossible.

They also fooled away an emperor's riches. For they promised to dig a navigable canal from Lake Avernus to the Tiber estuary, over the stony shore and mountain

---

* 418 years, 418 months, and 418 days had passed since the traditional date of the burning of Rome by the Gauls (390 BC).

barriers. The only water to feed the canal was in the Pontine marshes. Elsewhere, all was precipitous or waterless. Moreover, even if a passage could have been forced, the labour would have been unendurable and unjustified. But Nero was eager to perform the incredible; so he attempted to excavate the hills adjoining Lake Avernus. Traces of his frustrated hopes are visible today.

In parts of Rome unfilled by Nero's palace, construction was not – as after the burning by the Gauls – without plan or demarcation. Street-fronts were of regulated alignment, streets were broad, and houses built round courtyards. Their height was restricted, and their frontages protected by colonnades. Nero undertook to erect these at his own expense, and also to clear debris from building-sites before transferring them to their owners. He announced bonuses, in proportion to rank and resources, for the completion of houses and blocks before a given date. Rubbish was to be dumped in the Ostian marshes by corn-ships returning down the Tiber.

A fixed proportion of every building had to be massive, untimbered stone from Gabii or Alba (these stones being fireproof). Furthermore, guards were to ensure a more abundant and extensive public water-supply, hitherto diminished by irregular private enterprise. Householders were obliged to keep fire-fighting apparatus in an accessible place; and semi-detached houses were forbidden – they must have their own walls. These measures were welcomed for their practicality, and they beautified the new city. Some, however, believed that the old town's configuration had been healthier, since its narrow streets and high houses had provided protection against the burning sun, whereas now the shadowless open spaces radiated a fiercer heat.

So much for human precautions. Next came attempts to appease heaven. After consultation of the Sibylline books, prayers were addressed to Vulcan, Ceres, and Proserpina. Juno, too, was propitiated. Women who had been married were responsible for the rites – first on the Capitol, then at the nearest sea-board, where water was taken to sprinkle her temple and statue. Women with husbands living also celebrated ritual banquets and vigils.

But neither human resources, nor imperial munificence, nor appeasement of the gods, eliminated sinister suspicions that the fire had been instigated. To suppress this rumour, Nero fabricated scapegoats – and punished with every refinement the notoriously depraved Christians (as they were popularly called). Their originator, Christ, had been executed in Tiberius' reign by the governor of Judaea, Pontius Pilatus. But in spite of this temporary setback the deadly superstition had broken out afresh, not only in Judaea (where the mischief had started) but even in Rome. All degraded and shameful practices collect and flourish in the capital.

First, Nero had self-acknowledged Christians arrested. Then, on their information, large numbers of others were condemned – not so much for incendiarism as for their antisocial tendencies. Their deaths were made farcical. Dressed in wild animals' skins, they were torn to pieces by dogs, or crucified, or made into torches to be ignited after dark as substitutes for daylight. Nero provided his Gardens for the spectacle, and exhibited displays in the Circus, at which he mingled with the crowd – or stood in a chariot, dressed as a charioteer. Despite their guilt as Christians, and the ruthless punishment it deserved, the victims were pitied. For it was felt that they were being sacrificed to one man's brutality rather than to the national interest.

Meanwhile Italy was ransacked for funds, and the provinces were ruined – unprivileged and privileged communities alike. Even the gods were included in the looting. Temples at Rome were robbed, and emptied of the gold dedicated for the triumphs and vows, the ambitions and fears, of generations of Romans. Plunder from Asia and Greece included not only offerings but actual statues of the gods. Two agents were sent to these provinces. One, Acratus, was an ex-slave, capable of any depravity. The other, Secundus Carrinas, professed Greek culture, but no virtue from it percolated to his heart.

Seneca, rumour went, sought to avoid the odium of this sacrilege by asking leave to retire to a distant country retreat, and then – permission being refused – feigning a muscular complaint and keeping to his bedroom. According to some accounts one of his former slaves, Cleonicus by name, acting on Nero's orders, intended to poison Seneca but he escaped – either because the man confessed or because Seneca's own fears caused him to live very simply on plain fruit, quenching his thirst with running water.

At this juncture there was an attempted break-out by gladiators at Praeneste. Their army guards overpowered them. But the Roman public, as always terrified (or fascinated) by revolution, were already talking of ancient calamities such as the rising of Spartacus. Soon afterwards a naval disaster occurred. This was not on active service; never had there been such profound peace. But Nero had ordered the fleet to return to Campania by a fixed date regardless of weather. So, despite heavy seas the steersmen started from Formiae. But when they tried to round Cape Misenum a south-westerly gale drove them ashore near Cumae and destroyed numerous warships and smaller craft.

As the year ended omens of impending misfortune were widely rumoured – unprecedentedly frequent lightning; a comet (atoned for by Nero, as usual, by aristocratic blood); two-headed offspring of men and beasts, thrown into the streets or discovered among the offerings to those deities to whom pregnant victims are sacrificed. Near Placentia a calf was born beside the road with its head fastened to one of its legs. Soothsayers deduced that a new head was being prepared for the world – but that it would be neither powerful nor secret since it had been deformed in the womb and given birth by the roadside.

The Plot

The consuls for the following year were Aulus Licinius
Nerva Silanus Firmus Pasidienus and Marcus Julius
Vestinus Atticus. As soon as they had assumed office, a
conspiracy was hatched and instantly gained strength.
Senators and knights, officers, even women, competed
to join. They hated Nero; and they liked Gaius
Calpurnius Piso. His membership of the aristocratic
Calpurnian house linked him, on his father's side, with
many illustrious families. Among the masses, too, he
enjoyed a great reputation for his good qualities, real or
apparent. For he employed his eloquence to defend his
fellow-citizens in court; he was a generous friend –
and gracious and affable even to strangers; and he also
possessed the accidental advantages of impressive stature
and a handsome face. But his character lacked seriousness
or self-control. He was superficial, ostentatious, and
sometimes dissolute. But many people are fascinated
by depravity and disinclined for austere morals on the
throne. Such men found Piso's qualities attractive.

However, his ambitions were not what originated the
conspiracy. Who did, who initiated this enterprise which
so many joined, I could not easily say. Subrius Flavus, a
colonel of the Guard, and Sulpicius Asper, company-
commander, were in the forefront – as their courageous
deaths showed. Violent hatred was what brought in

Lucan and Plautius Lateranus. Lucan's animosity was personal. For Nero had the impudence to compete with Lucan as a poet, and had impeded his reputation by vetoing his publicity. Lateranus joined from no personal grievance; his motive was patriotism. Two other senators, Flavius Scaevinus and Afranius Quintianus, belied their reputations by becoming leaders in so important a project. For Scaevinus' brain was ruined by dissipation, and he led a languid sleepy life. Quintianus was a notorious degenerate who had been insulted by Nero in an offensive poem, and desired revenge.

These men talked to each other, and to their friends, about the emperor's crimes and his reign's imminent close. They were joined by seven Roman knights: Claudius Senecio, Cervarius Proculus, Volcacius Araricus, Julius Augurinus, Munatius Gratus, Antonius Natalis and Marcius Festus. Senecio was Nero's close associate, and so his position was especially perilous since they were still ostensibly friends. Natalis shared all Piso's secrets. The rest looked to revolution for personal advancement. Nor were Flavus and Asper the only officers involved. Other accomplices were the Guard colonels Gaius Gavius Silvanus and Statius Proxumus, and company-commanders, Maximus Scaurus and Venetus Paulus, were also in the plot. But the mainstay was felt to be Faenius Rufus, commander of the Guard. His respectability and good reputation had made less impression on Nero than the cruelty and depravity of his colleague Tigellinus – who persecuted Faenius with slanders, reiterating the alarming allegation that he had been Agrippina's lover and was intent on avenging her.

So when the conspirators were satisfied by Faenius' own repeated assurances that he was with them, serious discussion began about the date and place of Nero's murder. Subrius Flavus, it was said, had felt tempted to attack Nero when the emperor was singing on the stage or rushing from place to place during the night, unguarded, while his palace burned. Flavus had been attracted in the latter instance by Nero's opportune solitude, and in the former, conversely, by the large crowds which would witness the noble deed. But what held him back was that hindrance to all mighty enterprises, the desire for survival.

The plotters hesitated, still hoping and fearing. A woman called Epicharis, who had extracted their secret – it is not known how, for she had never before interested herself in anything good – kept urging them on and assailing them. Finally, happening to be in Campania and becoming impatient with the slowness of the conspirators, she attempted to unsettle and implicate the naval officers at Misenum. She began with a rear-admiral named Volusius Proculus, who had helped Nero with his mother's murder and felt his promotion had fallen short of so tremendous a crime. Whether their friendship was longstanding or recent is unknown. At all events Proculus told the woman of his services to Nero and their inadequate reward, and expressed not only discontent but the determination to have his own back if the chance occurred. This raised hopes that Proculus might be induced to act, and bring others in. The fleet could be extremely useful and provide valuable opportunities, since Nero enjoyed going to sea off Puteoli and Misenum.

So Epicharis went further. Enlarging on the emperor's abolition of the senate's rights and whole criminal record, she revealed the plan to avenge Rome's destruction at Nero's hands – only let Proculus make ready to do his part by winning over the best men, and he should be worthily rewarded. But she did not disclose the names of the conspirators. So, when Proculus proceeded – as he did – to report what he had heard to Nero, his information was useless. Epicharis was summoned and confronted with Proculus, but in the absence of witnesses easily refuted him. However, she herself was kept in custody. For Nero suspected that the story, though unproven, might not be untrue.

The conspirators were now tormented by fears of betrayal. They wanted to perform the assassination quickly – at Piso's villa at Baiae. For Nero appreciated its charms and often came for a bathe or banquet, without guards or imperial pomp. But Piso refused, arguing that to stain the sancity of hospitality with the blood of an emperor, however evil, would cause a bad impression. The city would be a better place, he said – that detested palace Nero had plundered his people to build; or, since their deed would be in the public interest, a public centre.

That was what Piso said aloud. But secretly he was afraid of a rival claimant to the throne – Lucius Junius Silanus Torquatus (II). The illustrious birth of Torquatus, and his upbringing by Gaius Cassius Longinus, fitted him for the highest destiny. Moreover non-conspirators, who might pity Nero as the victim of a crime, would back Torquatus readily. Some thought that Piso had also wished to prevent the lively consul, Marcus Julius Vestinus Atticus, from leading a Republican movement or insisting that the next emperor should be chosen by himself. For Vestinus was not one of the conspirators – though Nero used the charge to gratify his longstanding hatred of an innocent man.

They finally decided to execute their design at the Circus Games, on the day dedicated to Ceres. For though Nero rarely left the seclusion of his palace and gardens, he often attended Circus performances, and was more accessible in their festive atmosphere. The attack was planned as follows. Plautius Lateranus, ostensibly petitioning for financial assistance, was to prostrate himself before the unsuspecting emperor and then – being both resolute and muscular – bring him down and hold him. As Nero lay pinned down, the military men among the plotters, and any others sufficiently daring, would rush up and kill him. The leading role was claimed by Flavius Scaevinus, who had taken a dagger from a temple of Safety or (according to other reports) from the Shrine of Fortune at Ferentum, and wore it as the dedicated instrument of a great enterprise.

Meanwhile Piso was to wait at the temple of Ceres, from which Faenius Rufus and the rest were to fetch him to the Guards' camp. The elder Pliny adds that, to win popular favour for Piso, Claudius' daughter Claudia Antonia was to accompany him. True or false, I have felt that this statement ought at least to be recorded. Yet it seems absurd either that Claudia Antonia should have staked her name and life on so hopeless a project, or that

Piso, famous for his devotion to his wife, could have pledged himself to another marriage – unless indeed the lust for power outblazes all other feelings combined.

The secret was astonishingly well kept, considering the differences of the conspirators in social and financial position, rank, age, and sex. But betrayal came in the end – from the house of Flavius Scaevinus. The day before the attempt, he had a long conversation with Antonius Natalis. Then Scaevinus returned home and signed his will. Taking the aforesaid dagger from its sheath, and complaining that it was blunt with age, he gave it to his freed slave Milichus to be sharpened and polished on a stone. Then came a dinner-party, more luxurious than usual, at which Scaevinus freed his favourite slaves and gave others presents of money. He maintained a desultory conversation with superficial gaiety. But he was evidently anxious and seriously preoccupied. Finally, he instructed the same Milichus to prepare bandages and styptics for wounds.

Perhaps Milichus was in the secret, and had hitherto proved trustworthy. Alternatively (and this is the usual version) he knew nothing, but his suspicions were now aroused. At all events his slave's brain considered the rewards of treachery and conceived ideas of vast wealth and power. Then morality, his patron's life, gratitude for his freedom, counted for nothing. His wife's womanly, sordid advice implanted a further motive, fear. Many slaves and former slaves, she recalled, had been there and seen the same happenings – one man's silence would be useless, and the rewards would go to the informer who spoke first.

So at daybreak Milichus left for the Servilian Gardens. At first he was kept out. Finally, however, after insisting on the dreadful gravity of his news, he was taken by the doorkeepers to Nero's freed slave Epaphroditus – who conducted him to Nero. Milichus then revealed the resolute determination of the senators, the danger to Nero's life, and everything else he had heard or guessed. Exhibiting the dagger destined for Nero's murder, Milichus urged that the accused man be fetched. Scaevinus was arrested by soldiers. But he denied his guilt.

'The weapon concerned in the charge,' he said, 'is a venerated heirloom kept in my bedroom. This ex-slave Milichus has stolen it. As to my will, I have often signed new clauses without particularly noting the date. I have given slaves their freedom and money-gifts before. This time the scale was larger because, with reduced means and pressing creditors, I feared my will would be rejected. My table has always been generous, my life comfortable – too comfortable for austere critics. Bandages for wounds I did not order. But the man's allegations of patent untruths are so unconvincing that he has added this charge merely because it rests wholly on his own evidence.'

Scaevinus spiritedly reinforced this defence by assailing the ex-slave as an infamous rascal. His self-possessed tones and features would have annihilated the accusation if Milichus' wife had not reminded her husband that Scaevinus had spoken privately and at length with Antonius Natalis, and that both of them were associates of Gaius Calpurnius Piso. So Natalis was summoned, and he and Scaevinus were interrogated separately about their conversation and its subject. The discrepancy between their replies aroused suspicion, and they were put in chains.

At the threat and sight of torture they broke down – Natalis first. With his more intimate knowledge of the whole conspiracy (and greater cunning as an accuser), he began by denouncing Piso – then Seneca. Either Natalis had really acted as intermediary between Seneca and Piso or he hoped to conciliate Nero, who loathed Seneca and sought every means to destroy him. Scaevinus was equally unheroic – or he may have thought that since all was known silence held no advantages. At all events, when told of Natalis' confession, he named the remaining conspirators. Of these, Lucan, Afranius Quintianus, and Claudius Senecio long refused to incriminate themselves. But finally, tempted by a bribe of impunity, they confessed. What they said explained their hesitation, for Lucan denounced his own mother Acilia, and his two partners implicated their closest friends, Glitius Gallus and Annius Pollio.

Nero now remembered the information of Volusius Proculus and consequent arrest of Epicharis. Thinking no female body could stand the pain, he ordered her to be tortured. But lashes did not weaken her denials, nor did branding – nor the fury of the torturers at being defied by a woman. So the first day's examination was frustrated. Next day her racked limbs could not support her, so she was taken for further torments in a chair. But on the way she tore off her breast-band, fastened it in a noose to the chair's canopy, and placed her neck inside it. Then, straining with all her weight, she throttled the little life that was still in her. So, shielding in direst agony men unconnected with her and almost strangers, this former slavewoman set an example which particularly shone when free men, Roman knights and senators, were betraying, before anybody had laid a hand on them, their nearest and dearest. For Lucan and Senecio and Quintianus gave away their fellow-conspirators wholesale.

Nero became increasingly frightened. His guard had been redoubled. Indeed, the whole of Rome was virtually put in custody – troops manned the walls, and blockaded the city by sea and river. Roman public squares and homes, and even neighbouring towns and country districts, were invaded by infantry and cavalry. Among them were Germans; being foreigners, the emperor trusted them particularly.

Line after line of chained men were dragged to their destination at the gates of Nero's Gardens. When they were brought in to be interrogated, guilt was deduced from affability to a conspirator, or a chance conversation or meeting, or entrance to a party or a show together. Fierce interrogation by Nero and Tigellinus was supplemented by savage attacks from Faenius Rufus. No informer had denounced him yet; so, to establish his independence of his fellow-conspirators, he bullied them. When Subrius Flavius, who was standing by, inquired by a sign – in the middle of an actual trial – if he should draw his sword and assassinate Nero, Faenius Rufus shook his head and checked Subrius' impulse as his hand was already moving to the hilt.

After the betrayal of the plot, while Milichus was

talking and Scaevinus hesitating, Piso was urged to go to the Guards' camp and test the attitude of the troops, or mount the platform in the Forum and try the civilians. 'If your fellow-conspirators rally round you,' it was argued, 'outsiders will follow. Once a move is made the publicity will be immense – a vitally important point in revolutions. Nero has taken no precautions against this. Unforeseen developments intimidate even courageous men, so how could forcible counter-measures be feared from this actor – with Tigellinus and Tigellinus' mistresses as his escort! Many things that look hard to timid people can be done by trying.

'It is useless to expect loyal silence when so many accomplices are involved, body and soul. Tortures and rewards find a way anywhere. You too will be visited and put in chains – and ultimately to a degrading death. How much finer to die for the good of your country, calling for men to defend its freedom! The army may fail you, the people abandon you. But you yourself – if you must die early – die in a way of which your ancestors and posterity could approve!'

But Piso was unimpressed. After a brief public appearance, he shut himself in his house and summoned up courage for his end, waiting for the Guardsmen. Nero, suspicious of old soldiers as likely supporters of Piso, had selected new or recent recruits as his assassins. But Piso died by opening the veins in his arms. He loaded his will with repulsive flattery of Nero. This was done because Piso loved his own wife Satria Galla, though she was low-born and her beauty her only asset. He had stolen her from her former husband, a friend of his called

Domitius Silus, whose complaisance – like her miscon-
duct – had increased Piso's notoriety.

The next to be killed by Nero was the consul-designate
Plautius Lateranus. His removal was so hasty that he was
not allowed to embrace his children or given the customary short respite to choose his own death. Hurried off to
the place reserved for slaves' executions, Lateranus was
dispatched by a Guard colonel, Statius Proxumus. He
died in resolute silence – without denouncing the
officer's equal guilt.

Seneca's death followed. It delighted the emperor.
Nero had no proof of Seneca's complicity but was glad
to use arms against him when poison had failed. The
only evidence was a statement of Antonius Natalis that
he had been sent to visit the ailing Seneca and complain
because Seneca had refused to receive Piso. Natalis had
conveyed the message that friends ought to have friendly
meetings; and Seneca had answered that frequent meetings and conversations would benefit neither: but that
his own welfare depended on Piso's.

A colonel of the Guard, Gavius Silvanus, was ordered
to convey this report to Seneca and ask whether he
admitted that those were the words of Natalis and himself. Fortuitously or intentionally, Seneca had returned
that day from Campania and halted at a villa four miles
from Rome. Towards evening the officer arrived.
Surrounding the villa with pickets, he delivered the
emperor's message to Seneca as he dined with his wife
Pompeia Paulina and two friends. Seneca replied as
follows: 'Natalis was sent to me to protest, on Piso's
behalf, because I would not let him visit me. I answered

excusing myself on grounds of health and love of quiet. I could have had no reason to value any private person's welfare above my own. Nor am I a flatterer. Nero knows this exceptionally well. He has had more frankness than servility from Seneca!'

The officer reported this to Nero in the presence of Poppaea and Tigellinus, intimate counsellors of the emperor's brutalities. Nero asked if Seneca was preparing for suicide. Gavius Silvanus replied that he had noticed no signs of fear or sadness in his words or features. So Silvanus was ordered to go back and notify the death-sentence. According to Fabius Rusticus, he did not return by the way he had come but made a detour to visit the commander of the Guard, Faenius Rufus; he showed Faenius the emperor's orders, asking if he should obey them; and Faenius, with that ineluctable weakness which they all revealed, told him to obey. For Silvanus was himself one of the conspirators – and now he was adding to the crimes which he had conspired to avenge. But he shirked communicating or witnessing the atrocity. Instead he sent in one of his staff-officers to tell Seneca he must die.

Unperturbed, Seneca asked for his will. But the officer refused. Then Seneca turned to his friends. 'Being forbidden,' he said, 'to show gratitude for your services, I leave you my one remaining possession, and my best: the pattern of my life. If you remember it, your devoted friendship will be rewarded by a name for virtuous accomplishments.' As he talked – and sometimes in sterner and more imperative terms – he checked their tears and sought to revive their courage. Where had their philosophy gone, he asked, and that resolution against impending misfortunes which they had devised over so many years? 'Surely nobody was unaware that Nero was cruel!' he added. 'After murdering his mother and brother, it only remained for him to kill his teacher and tutor.'

These words were evidently intended for public hearing. Then Seneca embraced his wife and, with a tenderness very different from his philosophical imperturbability, entreated her to moderate and set a term to her grief, and take just consolation, in her bereavement, from contemplating his well-spent life. Nevertheless, she insisted on dying with him, and demanded the executioner's stroke. Seneca did not oppose her brave decision. Indeed, loving her wholeheartedly, he was reluctant to leave her behind to be persecuted. 'Solace in life was what I commended to you,' he said. 'But you prefer death and glory. I will not grudge your setting so fine an example. We can die with equal fortitude. But yours will be the nobler end.'

Then, each with one incision of the blade, he and his wife cut their arms. But Seneca's aged body, lean from austere living, released the blood too slowly. So he also severed the veins in his ankles and behind his knees. Exhausted by severe pain, he was afraid of weakening his wife's endurance by betraying his agony – or of losing his own self-possession at the sight of her sufferings. So he asked her to go into another bedroom. But even in his last moments his eloquence remained. Summoning secretaries, he dictated a dissertation. (It has been published in his own words, so I shall refrain from paraphrasing it.)

Nero did not dislike Paulina personally. In order, therefore, to avoid increasing his ill-repute for cruelty, he ordered her suicide to be averted. So, on instructions from the soldiers, slaves and ex-slaves bandaged her arms and stopped the bleeding. She may have been unconscious. But discreditable versions are always popular, and some took a different view – that as long as she feared there was no appeasing Nero, she coveted the distinction of dying with her husband, but when better prospects appeared life's attractions got the better of her. She lived on for a few years, honourably loyal to her husband's memory, with pallid features and limbs which showed how much vital blood she had lost.

Meanwhile Seneca's death was slow and lingering. Poison, such as was formerly used to execute State criminals at Athens, had long been prepared; and Seneca now entreated his experienced doctor Annaeus Statius, who was also an old friend, to supply it. But when it came, Seneca drank it without effect. For his limbs were already cold and numbed against the poison's action. Finally he was placed in a bath of warm water. He sprinkled a little of it on the attendant slaves, commenting that this was his libation to Jupiter. Then he was carried into a vapour-bath, where he suffocated. His cremation was without ceremony, in accordance with his own instructions about his death – written at the height of his wealth and power.

It was rumoured that Subrius Flavus and certain company-commanders of the Guard had secretly plotted, with Seneca's knowledge, that when Nero had been killed by Piso's agency Piso too should be murdered, and the throne given to Seneca: it would look as though men uninvolved in the plot had chosen Seneca for his moral qualities. Flavus was widely quoted as saying that, in point of disgrace, it made little difference to remove a lyre-player and replace him by a performer in tragedies. For Nero's singing to the lyre was paralleled by Piso's singing of tragic parts.

But the respite of the army conspirators was at an end. Finding Faenius Rufus' dual role as plotter and inquisitor intolerable, those who had turned informers longed to betray him. So while he pressed and threatened Scaevinus the latter retorted sneeringly that no one was better informed than Faenius himself – he should demonstrate his gratitude voluntarily to his excellent emperor. Words failed Faenius in reply. So did silence; a stammering utterance betrayed his terror. The remaining conspirators, especially the knight Cervarius Proculus, pressed for his conviction. The emperor ordered a soldier named Cassius, who was in attendance because of his great physical strength, to seize Faenius and bind him.

The evidence of the same fellow-conspirators next destroyed the Guard colonel Subrius Flavus. His first line of defence was difference of character: a soldier like him would never have shared such an enterprise with these effeminate civilians. But, when pressed, Flavus admitted his guilt, and gloried in it. Asked by Nero why he had forgotten his military oath, he replied: 'Because I detested you! I was as loyal as any of your soldiers as long as you deserved affection. I began detesting you when you murdered your mother and wife and became charioteer, actor, and incendiary!' I have given his actual words because they did not obtain the publicity of Seneca's; yet the soldier's blunt, forceful utterance was equally worth recording. Nothing in this conspiracy fell more shockingly on Nero's ears. For although ready enough to commit crimes, he was unaccustomed to be told about them.

A fellow-colonel, Veianius Niger, was detailed to execute Flavus. But when he ordered a grave to be dug in a field nearby, Flavus objected it was too shallow and narrow. 'More bad discipline,' he remarked to the soldiers in attendance. Then, bidden to offer his neck firmly, he replied: 'You strike equally firmly!' But the executioner, trembling violently, only just severed the head with two blows. However he boasted of his ferocity to Nero, saying he had killed Flavus with 'a stroke and a half!'

Another officer of the Guard, the company-commander Sulpicius Asper, was the next to show exemplary courage. For when Nero asked why he had plotted to kill him, Asper replied that it was the only way to rescue Nero from evil ways. He was convicted and executed. His equals likewise died without disgracing themselves. But Faenius Rufus was less brave – and could not keep lamentations even out of his will.

Nero was also expecting the incrimination of the consul Marcus Julius Vestinus Atticus, whom he regarded as revolutionary and disaffected. But none of the conspirators had confided in Vestinus. Some had long-standing feuds with him; others thought him impetuous and independent. Nero hated him as a result of their intimate association. For Vestinus knew and despised the emperor's worthlessness, while Nero feared this out-spoken friend, who made him the butt of crude jokes; when they are based on truth, they rankle. Besides, Vestinus had added a further motive by marrying Statilia Messalina, although he knew her to be one of Nero's mistresses. Yet no accuser came forward, and there was no charge.

So Nero could not assume the judge's role. Accordingly, he behaved like an autocrat instead, and sent a battalion of the Guard. Its commander, Gerellanus, was ordered to forestall the consul's designs, seize his 'citadel', and overpower his picked young followers. For the house where Vestinus lived overlooked the Forum, and he kept handsome slaves, all young. Vestinus had finished his consular duties for the day and was giving a dinner-party – unsuspecting, or pretending to be – when the soldiers entered and said the commander wanted him. He instantly rose and rapidly initiated all his arrangements. Shutting himself in his bedroom, he called his doctor and had his veins cut. Before the effects were felt, he was carried to a vapour-bath, and plunged into hot water. No word of self-pity escaped him. Meanwhile his dinner-companions were surrounded by Guardsmen and not released until late at night. It amused Nero to picture their expectation of death after dinner. But finally he ruled that they had been punished enough for their consular party.

Then he ordered Lucan to die. When he felt loss of blood numbing his feet and hands, and life gradually leaving his extremities (though his heart was still warm, and his brain clear), Lucan remembered verses he had written about a wounded soldier who had died a similar death. His last words were a recitation of this passage. Claudius Senecio, Afranius Quintianus, and Flavius Scaevinus were the next to die. Their deaths belied their effeminate lives. Then, without memorable words or actions, the remaining conspirators perished.

Executions now abounded in the city, and thank-offerings on the Capitol. Men who had lost their sons, or brothers, or other kinsmen, or friends, thanked the gods and decorated their houses with laurel, and fell before Nero, kissing his hand incessantly. Interpreting this as joy, he pardoned Antonius Natalis and Cervarius Proculus for their prompt information. Milichus was richly compensated, and adopted the Greek word for 'Saviour' as his name. One colonel of the Guard, Gavius Silvanus, was acquitted but killed himself, and another, Statius Proxumus, frustrated the imperial pardon by a melodramatic suicide. Four more, Pompeius, Cornelius Martialis, Flavius Nepos, and Statius Domitius, were deprived of their rank. They did not hate the emperor: but it was believed that they did.

Three unimplicated men, Decimus Novius Priscus, Glitius Gallus and Annius Pollio, were disgraced and exiled – the first of them because he was Seneca's friend. Priscus and Gallus were accompanied by their wives, Artoria Flaccilla and Egnatia Maximilla respectively. Egnatia's departure was to her credit, because her wealth was not confiscated – and its later confiscation did her credit too. Rufrius Crispinus was banished. The ostensible reason was conspiracy, but it was really because Nero hated him as Poppaea's ex-husband. Two more,

Verginius Flavus and Gaius Musonius Rufus, went because of their distinction as professors of rhetoric and philosophy. The massive list continues with five more: Cluvidienus Quietus, Julius Agrippa, Blitius Catulinus, Petronius Priscus, and Julius Altinus. They were permitted to live in the Aegean islands. Caesennius Maximus and Caedicia, the wife of Scaevinus, only learnt of their trial when they received their sentence: exclusion from Italy. Lucan's mother, Acilia, was ignored – unacquitted, but unpunished.

When this was all done, Nero addressed the Guard and presented each man with two thousand sesterces and free corn (they had hitherto paid the market price). Then, as though to announce a military victory, he summoned the senate and awarded honorary Triumphs to the former consul Publius Petronius Turpilianus, the praetor-designate Marcus Cocceius Nerva,* and the commander of the Guard Tigellinus. The two last were also awarded statues in the Palace, as well as triumphal effigies in the Forum. An honorary consulship was bestowed on Nymphidius Sabinus. This is his first appearance, so I must dwell on him for a moment – for he was to be deeply involved in Rome's imminent calamities. His mother was an attractive ex-slave who had hawked her charms among the slaves and freed slaves of emperors. His father, he claimed, was Gaius [Caligula]. For Nymphidius happened to be tall and grim-faced. And it was certainly possible that his mother had taken part in the amusements of Gaius, whose tastes ran to prostitutes.

* The future emperor Nerva (AD 96–8).

After his speech in the senate, Nero published an edict appending the statements of the informers and confessions of the convicted. For widespread popular attacks charged him with murdering even innocent men from jealousy or fear. However, the initiation, development, and suppression of the conspiracy are fully documented in reliable contemporary writings; and exiles who returned to Rome after Nero's death told the same story.

In the senate, there was abundant congratulation – especially from those with most to lament. Its manifestations included attacks on Lucius Annaeus Junius Gallio. Terrified by his brother Seneca's death and appealing for his life, Gallio was denounced as a public enemy and parricide. But the prosecutor, Salienus Clemens, had to bow to the senate's unanimous refusal to let him utilize – as it seemed – national misfortunes for private animosities by reviving brutal measures concerning matters settled or dismissed by the clemency of the emperor.

Then thank-offerings were decreed to the gods for miraculously uncovering the conspiracy: and particularly to the Sun – who has an ancient temple in the Circus Maximus (where the crime was planned). The Circus Games of Ceres were to be enlarged by additional horse-races. The month of April was to take Nero's name. A temple of Welfare was to be constructed, also a memorial in the temple from which Scaevinus had taken the dagger. Nero himself dedicated that weapon on the Capitol, to Jupiter 'Vindex' the Avenger. At the time this went unnoticed. But after the revolt of Gaius Julius Vindex it was interpreted as a sign portending future retribution.

I find in the senate's minutes that the consul-designate Gaius Anicius Cerealis proposed that a temple should be erected, as a matter of urgency, to the Divine Nero. The proposer meant to indicate that the emperor had transcended humanity and earned its worship. But Nero himself vetoed this in case the malevolent twisted it into an omen of his death. For divine honours are paid to emperors only when they are no longer among men.

Innocent Victims

But fortune was about to make a fool of Nero. For he credulously believed a lunatic Carthaginian named Caesellius Bassus. This man put faith in a dream, left for Rome, and bribed his way into the emperor's presence. Addressing Nero, he alleged the discovery on his estate of an immensely deep cave containing masses of gold, not in coin but in ancient, unworked bullion. There were ponderous ingots lying about and standing like columns, he said – all hidden centuries ago. His explanation of this windfall from antiquity was this: after her flight from Troy and foundation of Carthage, Phoenician Dido had hidden the treasure in case too much wealth might corrupt her young nation, or the already hostile Numidian kings, coveting the gold, might go to war.

Nero failed to check the man's credibility or to send investigators to confirm its truthfulness. Instead, his imagination exaggerated the report, and he dispatched men to fetch the spoils he believed were lying ready to hand. Warships were allocated, with picked rowers to accelerate their journey. This was the outstanding current subject of conversation. The public were optimistic, sensible people the reverse. It happened to be the year of the second five-yearly Neronian Games, and speakers, in their panegyrics of the emperor, made this a leading theme: 'Earth,' they said, 'is now producing not only her accustomed crops, not only gold mixed with other substances – she is teeming with a new kind of fertility! Wealth unsought is sent by the gods!' – and every other invention which eloquent sycophants could devise. They were confident of their imperial listener's credulity.

These vain hopes increased Nero's extravagance. Existing resources were squandered as though the material for many more years of wastefulness were now accessible. Indeed, he already drew on this imaginary treasure for free distributions; his expectation of wealth actually contributed to the national impoverishment. Meanwhile Bassus dug up his ground – and a wide area round about – declaring that this or that was the location of the promised cave. The soldiers accompanied him, together with a horde of rustics engaged to undertake the work. Finally, however, he recovered from his delusion – expressing amazement that, after all his other hallucinations had come true, this one alone had deceived him. He sought escape from his shame and fright in suicide. (According to other sources, he was arrested but soon released, his property however being confiscated in compensation for the imaginary Royal Treasure.)

The five-yearly Games were now close. The senate tried to avert scandal by offering the emperor, in advance, the first prize for song, and also conferred on him a crown 'for eloquence' to gloss over the degradation attaching to the stage. But Nero declared that there was no need for favouritism or the senate's authority; he would compete on equal terms and rely on the conscience of the judges to award him the prize he deserved. First he recited a poem on the stage. Then, when the crowd shouted that he should 'display all his accomplishments' (those were their actual words), he made a second *entrée* as a musician.

Nero scrupulously observed harpists' etiquette. When tired, he remained standing. To wipe away perspiration, he used nothing but the robe he was wearing. He allowed no moisture from his mouth or nose to be visible. At the conclusion, he awaited the verdict of the judges in assumed trepidation, on bended knee, and with a gesture of deference to the public. And the public at least, used to applauding the poses even of professional actors, cheered in measured, rhythmical cadences. They sounded delighted. Indeed, since the national disgrace meant nothing to them, perhaps they were.

But people from remote country towns of austere, old-fashioned Italy, or visitors from distant provinces on official or private business, had no experience of outrageous behaviour; they found the spectacle intolerable. Their unpractised hands tired easily and proved unequal to the degrading task, thereby disorganizing the expert applauders and earning many cuffs from the Guardsmen who, to prevent any momentary disharmony or silence, were stationed along the benches. Numerous knights, it is recorded, were crushed to death forcing their way up through the narrow exits against the crowd. Others, as they sat day and night, collapsed and died. For absence was even more dangerous than attendance, since there were many spies unconcealedly (and more still secretly) noting who was there – and noting whether their expressions were pleased or dissatisfied. Humble offenders received instant punishment.

Against important people the grudge was momentarily postponed, but paid later. Vespasian, the story went, nodded somnolently; he was reprimanded by an ex-slave called Phoebus, and only rescued by enlightened intercession. Nor was this the last time he was in peril. But his imperial destiny saved him.

Soon after the Games Poppaea died. She was pregnant, and her husband, in a chance fit of anger, kicked her. Some writers record that she was poisoned; but this sounds malevolent rather than truthful, and I do not believe it – for Nero wanted children and loved his wife. She was buried in the Mausoleum of Augustus. Her body was not cremated in the Roman fashion, but was stuffed with spices and embalmed in the manner of foreign potentates. At the State funeral, Nero mounted the platform to praise her looks, her parenthood of an infant now deified, and her other lucky assets which could be interpreted as virtues.

Publicly Poppaea's death was mourned. But those who remembered her immorality and cruelty welcomed it. However, Nero's action caused disgust, which was accentuated when he forbade Gaius Cassius Longinus to attend the funeral. This was the first sign of impending trouble: and it came quickly. Lucius Junius Silanus Torquatus (II) became involved. His only offence was to be a respectable young member of the highest nobility; those of Cassius were his remarkable ancestral wealth and outstanding character. Nero wrote to the senate requesting that both should be expelled from public life. He charged Cassius with revering, among the statues of his ancestors, a representation of Gaius Cassius, labelled

'Leader of the Cause'* – thus planting the seeds of civil war and treason to the house of the Caesars.

But (the emperor added) a hated name was not enough material for revolution, so Cassius had taken on the unbalanced young nobleman Lucius Silanus as the rebellion's figurehead. Then Nero attacked Silanus (as he had earlier attacked his uncle, Decimus Junius Silanus Torquatus) for already allocating imperial responsibilities by designating his ex-slaves Financial Secretary, Petitions Secretary, and Secretary-General. The charge was fatuous. It was also untrue. For Silanus, besides feeling the effects of the prevalent terror, had been frightened by his uncle's death into extreme caution. Next, so-called informers fabricated against Cassius' wife, Junia Lepida, accusations of black magic and incest with her brother's son – Lucius Silanus. Two senators, Volcacius Tertullinus and Cornelius Marcellus, and a knight, Gaius Calpurnius Fabatus, were charged with complicity. But they avoided imminent condemnation by appealing to Nero. For he was preoccupied with important crimes, and they were eventually saved by their insignificance.

For Cassius and Silanus, the senate decreed banishment. Concerning Junia Lepida the emperor was to decide. Cassius was deported to Sardinia, where old age was left to do its work. Silanus was first removed to Ostia, with Naxos as his supposed destination; but he was instead confined in the Apulian country town of Barium. There, as he philosophically endured his thoroughly undeserved

* The inscribed bust was of Julius Caesar's assassin, whose full name was likewise Gaius Cassius Longinus.

misfortune, a company-commander of the Guard was sent to kill him. Seized and told to open his veins, he answered that he was ready to die but would not excuse his assassin the glorious duty. The officer, however, noting that though unarmed he was very strong and far from intimidated, ordered his men to overpower him. Silanus did not fail to resist, hitting back as much as his bare hands allowed. Finally the commander's sword struck him down, and he fell, wounded in front, as in battle.

Lucius Antistius Vetus, and his mother-in-law Sextia and daughter Antistia Pollitta, died just as courageously. All three appeared detestable to the emperor as living reproaches for his murder of Vetus' son-in-law, Rubellius Plautus. A chance for Nero to display his brutality was afforded by a former slave of Vetus named Fortunatus. This person, after stealing his patron's money, turned accuser, mobilizing an individual named Claudius Demianus who had been imprisoned for criminal actions by Vetus during his governorship of Asia but subsequently released by Nero as a reward for this accusation. When Vetus heard this, and knew he had to face the ex-slave on equal terms, he withdrew to his estate at Formiae, under secret military surveillance.

With him was his daughter. Besides the imminent peril, she was embittered by sorrow. This had lasted unceasingly ever since she had seen her husband Rubellius Plautus assassinated. She had clasped his bleeding neck, and kept his bloodstained clothes – an unkempt widow grieving incessantly, eating barely enough to stay alive. Now, at her father's plea, she went to Neapolis. Refused access to Nero, she lay in wait for him at the door. When he came, she entreated him to hear an innocent man, and not surrender his former fellow-consul to a man who had been a slave. She cried like a woman. She also screamed in unwomanly fury. But appeals and reproaches alike left the emperor cold.

So she sent her father word to abandon hope and accept the inevitable. Simultaneously there came forewarning of a trial in the senate, and a harsh verdict. Some advised Vetus to name the emperor as his principal heir, thus securing the residue for his grandchildren. But he scorned to spoil what had mostly been a life of freedom by servility at its close. So he distributed his ready cash among his slaves, and bade them remove everything portable for themselves, keeping only three couches for the end.

Then, in one room, with a single weapon, all three of them – Vetus, his mother-in-law, and his daughter – opened their veins. Wearing a single garment each for decency's sake, they were hastily carried into the bath. The young woman gazed long at her father and grandmother, and they at her. All three prayed to cease their feeble breathing speedily and be the first to die – but not be long outlived. Fate observed the right order. First the two eldest perished, then the young Antistia. After burial, they were denounced, and condemned to punishment in the ancient fashion. Nero intervened, allowing them to die unsupervised. But this farce was subsequent to their deaths.

A knight called Publius Gallus was outlawed for being on good terms with Vetus as well as a close friend of Faenius Rufus. The ex-slave who had preferred the charge against Vetus was rewarded by a seat in the theatre among the attendants of the tribunes. The names of the months following 'Neroneus' – otherwise April – were changed. May became 'Claudius', June 'Germanicus'. According to the originator of the proposal, Servius Cornelius Orfitus by name, the latter change was necessary because the execution of two Junii Torquati had made the name 'June' ill-omened.

Heaven, too, marked this crime-stained year with tempest and pestilence. Campania was ravaged by a hurricane which destroyed houses, orchards, and crops over a wide area and almost extended its fury to the city. At Rome, a plague devastated the entire population. No miasma was discernible in the air. Yet the houses were full of corpses, and the streets of funerals. Neither sex nor age conferred immunity. Slave or free, all succumbed just as suddenly. Their mourning wives and children were often cremated on the very pyres by which they had sat and lamented. Senators and knights were not spared. But their deaths seemed less tragic; for by dying like other men they merely seemed to be forestalling the emperor's blood-thirstiness.

In this year the Roman army in the Illyrian provinces, weakened by discharges due to age and unfitness, was replenished by recruiting in Narbonese Gaul, Africa, and Asia.

A disastrous fire at Lugdunum was alleviated by an imperial gift of four million sesterces to repair the town's damage – the same sum as its people had contributed to Rome's similar misfortunes.

★

When, in the following year, Gaius Suetonius Paulinus and Gaius Luccius Telesinus became consuls, Antistius Sosianus, who, as I have mentioned, was in exile for writing offensive poems about Nero, noted the rewards paid to informers and the emperor's readiness for bloodshed. A restless opportunist by nature, he utilized the similarity of their fortunes to make friends with a fellow-exile at the same place, called Pammenes. The latter's fame as an astrologer had won him many friends. Sosianus noted that messengers were continually arriving to consult him – and deduced that there must be a purpose behind their visits.

He also learnt that Pammenes received an annual subsidy from Publius Anteius. Nero hated Anteius (Sosianus knew) as a friend of Agrippina, and might well covet his wealth – a frequent cause of fatalities. Sosianus therefore intercepted a letter from Anteius. He also stole from Pammenes' secret files documents giving Anteius' horoscope and destiny. He likewise found there papers relating to the birth and life of Marcus Ostorius Scapula. Then he wrote to the emperor, intimating that, if he were granted a brief respite from his banishment, he would bring information vital to Nero's safety. For Anteius and Ostorius, he said, were studying their own and the emperor's destinies – and thus imperilling the empire.

Fast ships were immediately sent, and Sosianus was soon there. When his denunciation became known, Anteius and Ostorius were regarded less as defendants than as persons already condemned. Indeed, no one would witness Anteius' will until Tigellinus sanctioned this – after warning the testator to complete the formalities speedily. Anteius took poison, but impatient with its slowness obtained a quicker death by cutting his veins.

Ostorius was at the time at a remote estate on the Ligurian border. There a staff-officer of the Guard was dispatched to kill him rapidly. The reason for this haste was Nero's fear of a personal attack. Always cowardly, he was more terrified than ever since the recently discovered conspiracy. Besides, Ostorius was of huge physique and an expert with weapons – his distinguished military record included the oak-wreath for saving a citizen's life in Britain. The officer arrived; and closing every exit from the house, he told Ostorius of the emperor's orders. The courage he had often demonstrated against the enemy Ostorius turned upon himself. Because his veins, when opened, let the blood out too slowly, he ordered a slave to hold up his hand firmly with a dagger in it – nothing more. Then Ostorius pulled the slave's hand on to his own throat.

Even if I were describing foreign wars and patriotic deaths, this monotonous series of events would have become tedious both for me and for my readers. For I should expect them to feel as surfeited as myself by the tragic sequence of citizen deaths – even if they had been honourable deaths. But this slavish passivity, this torrent of wasted bloodshed far from active service, wearies, depresses, and paralyses the mind. The only indulgence I would ask the reader for the inglorious victims is that he should forbear to censure them. For the fault was not theirs. The cause was rather heaven's anger with Rome – and not an isolated burst of anger such as could be passed over with a single mention, as when armies are defeated or cities captured. And let us at least make this concession to the reputation of famous men: just as in the manner of their burial they are distinguished from the common herd, so when their deaths are mentioned let each receive his separate, permanent record.

Within a few days there fell, one after another, Annaeus Mela, Gaius Anicius Cerealis, Rufrius Crispinus, and Petronius. Mela and Crispinus were Roman knights who enjoyed the status of senators. The latter, formerly commander of the Guard – and an honorary consul – but recently exiled to Sardinia on a charge of conspiracy, received the order to die, and committed suicide. Mela, brother of Seneca and of Lucius Annaeus Junius Gallio, had refrained from seeking office owing to his perverse ambition to achieve a consul's influence while remaining a knight. He had also seen a shorter road to wealth in becoming an agent handling the emperor's business. The fact that he was Lucan's father greatly enhanced his reputation. But after his son's death Mela called in Lucan's debts so harshly that one of the latter's intimate friends, Fabius Romanus, denounced him, fabricating a charge that father and son had shared complicity in the plot. The evidence was a forged letter from Lucan, which Nero examined: then he sent it to Mela, whose wealth he coveted.

Mela died in the fashionable way, opening his veins. First, however, he recorded large bequests to Tigellinus and the latter's son-in-law Cossutianus Capito – hoping to save the residue. He added a postscript protesting against his unfair fate, and contrasting his undeserved death with the survival of Crispinus and Cerealis, the emperor's enemies. But the postscript was regarded as a fabrication, Crispinus figuring because capital punishment had already been inflicted on him, and Cerealis to ensure its infliction. Soon afterwards Cerealis duly committed suicide – less pitied than the rest, because he was remembered to have betrayed a conspiracy to Gaius.

Petronius* deserves a brief obituary. He spent his days sleeping, his nights working and enjoying himself. Others achieve fame by energy, Petronius by laziness. Yet he was not, like others who waste their resources, regarded as dissipated or extravagant, but as a refined voluptuary. People liked the apparent freshness of his unconventional and unselfconscious sayings and doings. Nevertheless, as governor of Bithynia and later as consul, he had displayed a capacity for business.

Then, reverting to a vicious or ostensibly vicious way of life, he had been admitted into the small circle of Nero's intimates, as Arbiter of Taste: to the blasé emperor nothing was smart and elegant unless Petronius had given it his approval. So Tigellinus, loathing him as a rival and a more expert hedonist, denounced him on the grounds of his friendship with Flavius Scaevinus. This appealed to the emperor's outstanding passion – his cruelty. A slave was bribed to incriminate Petronius. No defence was heard. Indeed, most of his household were under arrest.

The emperor happened to be in Campania. Petronius too had reached Cumae; and there he was arrested.

---

* This Petronius 'Arbiter' was very probably the author of the earliest surviving Latin novel, the *Satyricon*.

Delay, with its hopes and fears, he refused to endure. He severed his own veins. Then, having them bound up again when the fancy took him, he talked with his friends – but not seriously, or so as to gain a name for fortitude. And he listened to them reciting, not discourses about the immortality of the soul or philosophy, but light lyrics and frivolous poems. Some slaves received presents – others beatings. He appeared at dinner, and dozed, so that his death, even if compulsory, might look natural.

Even his will deviated from the routine death-bed flatteries of Nero, Tigellinus, and other leaders. Petronius wrote out a list of Nero's sensualities – giving names of each male and female bed-fellow and details of every lubricious novelty – and sent it under seal to Nero. Then Petronius broke his signet-ring, to prevent its subsequent employment to incriminate others. Nero could not imagine how his nocturnal ingenuities were known. He suspected Silia, a woman of note (she was a senator's wife) who knew all his obscenities from personal experience – and was a close friend of Petronius. For breaking silence about what she had seen and known, she was exiled. Here the grievance was Nero's own. It was to Tigellinus' malevolence, however, that he sacrificed a former praetor, Minucius Thermus (II). A freed slave made criminal charges against this man; the ex-slave's penalty was torture, the patron's an undeserved death.

After the massacre of so many distinguished men, Nero finally coveted the destruction of Virtue herself by killing Thrasea and Marcius Barea Soranus. He had long hated them both. Against Thrasea there were additional motives. He had, as I mentioned, walked out of the senate during the debate about Agrippina. He had also been inconspicuous at the Youth Games. This gave all the more offence because during Games (the festival instituted by Antenor the Trojan) at his birthplace, Patavium, he had participated by singing in tragic costume. Besides, on the day when the praetor Antistius Sosianus was virtually condemned to death for writing offensive verses about Nero, he had proposed and carried a more lenient sentence. Again, after Poppaea's death, he had deliberately stayed away when divine honours were voted to her, and was not present at her funeral.

Cossutianus Capito kept these memories fresh. For that criminal bore Thrasea a grudge for helping a Cilician deputation to convict him for extortion. So now Capito added further charges: 'At the New Year, Thrasea evaded the regular oath. Though a member of the Board of Fifteen for Religious Ceremonies, he absented himself from the national vows. He has never sacrificed for the emperor's welfare or his divine voice. Once an indefatigable and invariable participant in the senate's discussions – taking sides on even the most trivial proposal – now, for three years, he has not entered the senate. Only yesterday, when there was universal competition to strike down Lucius Junius Silanus Torquatus (II) and Lucius Antistius Vetus, he preferred to take time off helping his dependants.

'This is party-warfare against the government. It is secession. If many more have the same impudence, it is war. As this faction-loving country once talked of Caesar versus Cato, so now, Nero, it talks of you versus Thrasea. And he has his followers – or his courtiers rather. They do not yet imitate his treasonable voting. But they copy his grim and gloomy manner and expression: they rebuke your amusements. He is the one man to whom your safety is immaterial, your talents unadmired. He dislikes the emperor to be happy. But even your unhappiness, your bereavements, do not appease him. Disbelief in Poppaea's divinity shows the same spirit as refusing allegiance to the acts of the divine Augustus and divine Julius. Thrasea rejects religion, abrogates law.

'In every province and army the official Gazette is read with special care – to see what Thrasea has refused to do. If his principles are better, let us adopt them. Otherwise, let us deprive these revolutionaries of their chief and champion. This is the school which produced men like Quintus Aelius Tubero and Marcus Favonius – unpopular names even in the old Republic. They acclaim Liberty to destroy the imperial régime. Having destroyed it, they will strike at Liberty too. Your removal of a Cassius was pointless if you propose to allow emulators of the Brutuses to multiply and prosper. Finally – write no instructions about Thrasea yourself. Leave the senate to decide between us.' Nero whipped up Cossutianus' hot temper still further, and associated with him the bitingly eloquent Titus Clodius Eprius Marcellus.

The prosecution of Marcius Barea Soranus had been claimed by Ostorius Sabinus, a knight, on the grounds of alleged incidents during the defendant's governorship of Asia. The energy and fairness of Barea Soranus in that post had increased the emperor's malevolence. He had industriously cleared the harbour of Ephesus, and had refrained from punishing Pergamum for forcibly pre-

venting an ex-slave of Nero called Acratus from removing its statues and pictures. However the charges against
him were friendship with Rubellius Plautus and courting
the provincials with revolutionary intentions. His conviction was timed just before Tiridates' arrival to receive
the Armenian crown. This was to divert attention from
domestic outrages to foreign affairs – or, perhaps, to
display imperial grandeur to the visitor by a truly royal
massacre of distinguished men.

All Rome turned out to welcome the emperor and
inspect the king. Thrasea's presence, however, was forbidden. Undismayed, he wrote to Nero inquiring what
the charges against him were and insisting that he would
clear himself if he were told them and given an opportunity to dispose of them. Nero took the letter eagerly,
hoping Thrasea had been frightened into some humiliat-
ing statement that would enhance the imperial prestige.
But this was not so. Indeed, it was Nero who took fright,
at the innocent Thrasea's spirited independence; so he
convened the senate.

Thrasea consulted his friends whether he should
attempt or disdain to defend himself. The advice he
received was contradictory. Some said he should attend
the senate. 'We know you will stand firm,' they said.
'Everything you say will enhance your renown! A secret
end is for the feeble-spirited and timid. Let the people
see a man who can face death. Let the senate hear
inspired, superhuman utterances. Even Nero might be
miraculously moved. But if his brutality persists, at least
posterity will distinguish a noble end from the silent,
spiritless deaths we have been seeing.'

The Madness of Nero

Other friends, while equally complimentary to himself, urged him to wait at home, forecasting jeers and insults if he attended the senate. 'Avert your ears from taunts and slanders,' they advised. 'Cossutianus and Eprius are not the only criminals. Others are savage enough not to stop at physical violence – and fear makes even decent men follow their lead. You have been the senate's glory. Spare them this degrading crime: leave their verdict on Thrasea uncertain. To make Nero ashamed of his misdeeds is a vain hope. Much more real is the danger of his cruelty to your wife and daughter and other dear ones. No – die untarnished, unpolluted, as gloriously as those in whose footsteps and precepts you have lived!'

One of those present, the fervent young Lucius Junius Arulenus Rusticus, sought glory by proposing, as tribune, to veto the senate's decree. Thrasea rejected his enthusiastic plan as futile – fatal to its author, and not even any help to the accused. 'My time is finished,' he said. 'I must not abandon my longstanding, unremitting way of life. But you are starting your official career. Your future is uncompromised, so you must consider carefully beforehand what political cause you intend to adopt in such times.' The advisability of his own presence or absence he reserved for personal decision.

Next morning, two battalions of the Guard, under arms, occupied the temple of Venus Genetrix. The approach to the senate-house was guarded by guards in civilian clothes displaying their swords. Troops too were arrayed round the principal forums and the law-courts. Under their menacing glares, the senators entered the building. The emperor's address was read by his quaestor. Without mentioning any name he rebuked members for neglecting their official duties and setting the knights a slovenly example. What wonder, he said, if senators from distant provinces stayed away, when many exconsuls and priests showed greater devotion to the embellishment of their gardens?

The accusers seized the weapon which this gave them. Cossutianus began the attack. Eprius Marcellus, following with even greater violence, claimed that the issue was one of prime national importance. The emperor's indulgence, he said, was hampered by the insubordination of those beneath him, and the senate had hitherto been over-lenient. 'For you have allowed yourselves,' he said, 'to be ridiculed with impunity – by the rebellious Thrasea, his equally infatuated son-in-law Helvidius Priscus (II), Gaius Paconius Agrippinus (heir to his father's hatred of emperors), and that scribbler of detestable verses Curtius Montanus. I insist that a former consul should attend the senate; a priest take the national vows; a citizen swear the oath of allegiance. Or has Thrasea renounced our ancestral customs and rites in favour of open treachery and hostility?

'In a word: let this model senator, this protector of the emperor's critics, appear and specify the reforms and changes that he wants. His detailed carpings would be more endurable than the universal censure of his silence. Does world-peace give him no satisfaction, or victories won without a Roman casualty? Do not gratify the perverted ambitions of a man who deplores national success, thinks of courts, theatres, and temples as deserts

– and threatens to exile himself. Here is a man to whom senatorial decrees, public office, Rome itself, mean not a thing. Let him sever all connection with the place he has long since ceased to love, and has now ceased even to honour with his attendance!'

While Eprius Marcellus spoke in this vein, grim and blustering as ever, fanatical of eye, voice, and features, the senators did not feel any genuine sadness: repeated perils had made the whole business all too familiar. And yet as they saw the Guardsmen's hands on their weapons, they felt a new, sharper terror. They thought of Thrasea's venerable figure. Some also pitied Helvidius, to suffer for his guiltless marriage relationship. And what was there against Agrippinus except his father's downfall? – for he too, though as innocent as his son, had succumbed to imperial cruelty under Tiberius. The worthy young Montanus, too, was no libellous poet. The cause of his banishment was his manifest talent.

Next Ostorius Sabinus, the accuser of Barea Soranus, entered and began to speak. He denounced the defendant's friendship with Rubellius Plautus, and claimed that Barea's governorship of Asia had been planned not to serve the public interest but to win popularity for himself – by encouraging the cities to rebellion. That was stale. But there was also a new charge involving Barea's daughter, Servilia, in his ordeal. She was said to have given large sums to magicians. This was true; but the cause was filial affection. Young and imprudent, she had consulted the magicians out of love for her father – but only about the prospects of her family's survival, and of Nero's compassion, and of a happy outcome to the senate's investigation. So she too was summoned before the senate. There, at opposite ends of the consul's dais, stood the elderly father and his teenage daughter, unconsolable for the loss of her exiled husband Annius Pollio – and unable even to look at her father, whose perils she had clearly intensified.

The accuser demanded whether she had sold her *trousseau* and taken the necklace from her neck in order to raise money for magical rites. At first she collapsed on the ground, weeping incessantly and not answering. But then she grasped the altar and its steps, and cried: 'Never have I called upon forbidden gods or spells! My unhappy prayers have had a single aim: that you, Caesar, and you, senators, should spare my dear father. I gave my jewels and clothes – the things that a woman in my position owns – as I would have given my blood and my life if the magicians had wanted them! I did not know the men before. They must answer for their own reputations and methods; that is not for me to do. I never mentioned the emperor except as a god. And everything was done without my poor father's knowledge. If it was a crime, I alone am to blame!'

Soranus broke in with the plea that she had not gone with him to the province, was too young to have known Rubellius Plautus, and was unimplicated in the charges against her husband. 'Her only crime is too much family affection,' he urged. 'Take her case separately – for me any fate will be acceptable.' Then he moved towards his daughter to embrace her, and she towards him. But attendants intervened and kept them apart.

Evidence was then heard. The brutality of the

prosecution aroused compassion – which was only equalled by the indignation felt against one of the witnesses, Publius Egnatius Celer. He was a dependant of Soranus bribed to ruin his friend. Though professing the Stoic creed, he was crafty and deceitful at heart, using a practised demeanour of rectitude as a cover for viciousness and greed. But money was capable of stripping off the mask. Egnatius became a standard warning that men of notorious depravity or obvious deceit yield nothing in nastiness to hypocritical pseudo-philosophers and treacherous friends. However, the same day provided a model of integrity – Cassius Asclepiodotus, the richest man in Bithynia. Having honoured Soranus when he prospered, he would not desert him in his fall. So he was deprived of his whole fortune and ordered into exile – thus affording a demonstration of heaven's impartiality between good and evil.

Thrasea, Soranus, and Servilia were allowed to choose their own deaths. Helvidius and Paconius were banned from Italy. Montanus was spared for his father's sake, with the stipulation that his official career should be discontinued. The accusers Eprius and Cossutianus received five million sesterces each, Ostorius twelve hundred thousand and an honorary quaestorship.

The consul's quaestor, sent to Thrasea, found him in the evening in his garden. In his company were numerous distinguished men and women. His attention, however, was concentrated on a Cynic professor, Demetrius. To judge from Thrasea's earnest expression, and audible snatches of their conversation, they were discussing the nature of the soul and the dichotomy of spirit and body.

A close friend, Domitius Caecilianus, came and informed him of the senate's decision. Thrasea urged the weeping and protesting company to leave rapidly and avoid the perils of association with a doomed man. His wife Arria, like Arria her mother, sought to share his fate. But he told her to stay alive and not deprive their daughter of her only protection.

Thrasea walked to the colonnade. There the quaestor found him, happy rather than sorrowful, because he had heard that his son-in-law Helvidius Priscus was merely banned from Italy. Then, taking the copy of the senate's decree, he led Helvidius and Demetrius into his bedroom, and offered the veins of both his arms. When the blood began to flow, he sprinkled it on the ground, and called the quaestor nearer. 'This is a libation,' he said, 'to Jupiter the Liberator. Look, young man! For you have been born (may heaven avert the omen!) into an age when examples of fortitude may be a useful support.'

Then, as his lingering death was very painful, he turned to Demetrius . . .

[The text of the *Annals* breaks off here.]